CHAOS to CALM

CHAOS to CALM

How to Reset Your Life and Manifest Your Dreams

Jackie Reeves
Founder of Soul Pathfinder Coaching

Copyright © 2025 by Jackie Reeves

All rights reserved. No part of this publication may be reproduced, distributed or transmitted in anyform or by any means without permission of the publisher, except in the case of brief quotations referencing the body of work and in accordance with copyright law.

The information given in this book should not be treated as a substitute for professional medical advice; always consult a medical practitioner. Any use of information in this book is at the reader's discretion and risk. Neither the author nor the publisher can be held responsible for any loss, claim or damage arising out of the use, or misuse, of the suggestions made, the failure to take medical advice of for any material on third party websites.

ISBN 978-1-916529-40-3 Paperback

ISBN 978-1-916529-41-0 Ebook

The Unbound Press
www.theunboundpress.com

Hey unbound one!

Welcome to this magical book brought to you by The Unbound Press.

At The Unbound Press we believe that when women write freely from the fullest expression of who they are, it can't help but activate a feeling of deep connection and transformation in others. When we come together, we become more and we're changing the world, one book at a time!

This book has been carefully crafted by both the author and publisher with the intention of inspiring you to move ever more deeply into who you truly are.

We hope that this book helps you to connect with your Unbound Self and that you feel called to pass it on to others who want to live a more fully expressed life.

With much love,
Nicola Humber

Founder of The Unbound Press

www.theunboundpress.com

This book is dedicated firstly to my loving husband and my best friend, Tony, on this adventure we call life. Thank you for supporting me, cheering me on and believing in me throughout writing this book.

Thank you, Universe, for opening my door to the happiness, health, abundance and joy that this work gives me in healing others and finding their unique path to happiness.

Contents

Introduction: Gentle Trigger Warning - xi

Introduction - xv

1. How it All Began - 1
2. The Determination Years - 19
3. The Newcastle Years - 25
4. Going Backwards to Come Forward - 47
5. Moving on to Pastures New - 67
6. Completion and Change - 79
7. Friendships Revisited, Renewed and Completed - 85
8. The Transition Years: Giving up – Getting up - 97
9. The Universe Gave Me a Wakeup Call - 107
10. Discovering ME - 117
11. Repeating Old Patterns One Last Time - 129
12. Lessons in Love - 141
13. The Growing Years - 161
14. Adventures in Hypnotherapy - 169
15. Moving On – Changing Lanes - 177
16. There Is No Wrong Decision - 181
17. My Path from Lockdown to Freedom - 191
18. The Gift - 201
19. Message Received - 211
20. The Key Ingredients to Make Lasting Change - 217

Chaos to Calm: The Toolbox Section - 244

How to Keep in Touch - 305

About the Author - 307

Introduction to my book Gentle Trigger Warning

Heart to Heart Before We Begin

Listen, this book is more than just pages – it's a journey we're about to take together.

A quick heads up: We're going to talk about some of life's messy, beautiful, complicated stuff. If you're in a tender place right now, that's okay. This book is not about reopening wounds – it's about healing, growing, and discovering how incredibly powerful you are.

Think of this as sitting down with a friend who's going to share some real, raw moments of life. Some stories might give you goosebumps, some might make you tear up, or some may invoke other emotions. This will absolutely light a fire of hope inside you.

Take what serves you. Leave what doesn't. There's no pressure, no judgment — just an invitation to explore, breathe, and maybe see yourself a little differently.

Ready to turn the page? Let's do this – together.

Imagine standing at the edge of your own possibility – breathless, curious, and just a little bit afraid.

This isn't just another self-help book. This is your personal revolution wrapped in pages.

I've been where you are right now. Feeling stuck. Overwhelmed. Wondering if something more is possible. I've walked that road and I'm about to show you that not only is transformation possible, but it's also inevitable when you have the right map.

What if I told you that the most powerful change happens not in grand, sweeping moments, but in quiet, deliberate choices? That every single challenge you've faced has been preparing you for something extraordinary?

Together, we'll navigate the intricate landscape of personal transformation. I'm not here to fix you (because you're not broken). I'm here to remind you of the incredible resilience that's been inside you all along.

Think of this as a conversation between two souls who are ready to break free from what's been holding them back. No judgment. No filters. Just raw, powerful possibility.

Introduction

Are you ready to shatter the chains of chaos that hold you back, and discover the extraordinary power within you?

Imagine stepping into a world where the storm within you transforms into a tranquil sea, where every challenge becomes an opportunity, and where your deepest desires are within reach. This is not just a dream, this is the magic that lies dormant within you, waiting to find that missing piece to your true path.

In the pages ahead, I invite you on an extraordinary journey where emotions, psychology, and spirituality merge into a powerful force.

My mission is to share my personal journey with you, unfolding my lessons so you can see the possibilities available for you to do the same. I want to awaken the energy that lies within to ignite this, so you move forward, reclaiming control over your life even when it feels like the world is overwhelming and spiralling out of control.

The question is, are you ready to let this transformation unfold? If so, let's embark on this life-altering voyage.

The Catalyst Book

Have you ever encountered a person, a moment, or a book that altered the course of your life? For me, it was one powerful book that sparked a profound shift, opening my mind to new possibilities and a new path. That book was the catalyst for my transformation, and now I'm eager to share that journey and the wisdom I gained with you.

This book is more than a memoir. It's a blueprint for transformation. It's about shifting from the draining frequency of chaos to the vibrant frequency of possibility. It's about realising that you have the power to create the life you've always wanted. Through my story, you'll discover the tools and techniques that guided me, lighting the way toward lasting change, emotional healing, and true happiness.

Join me as we navigate this journey together, from chaos to calm, and unleash the inner power that will lead you to fast-track your transformation – because the life you deserve is waiting just on the other side of this journey.

Are you ready to step into this new reality? Are you prepared to let this magic unfold and lead you to a life beyond your wildest imagination? If your answer is yes, then let the Voyage begin…

Chapter One
How it All Began

My life suddenly changed on the 19th of December 2001, when fire ripped through the ground floor of my little council house.

The following morning, as I wandered through the blackened remains of my possessions, I noticed something amazing.

There on the floor, lay a book.

It was a little smoke-damaged, but unbelievably it was the only thing that had survived...

It was a book that I had bought just the day before...

This one book changed my life.

This singular book became the catalyst for a transformation that defied the ashes of my past. But to comprehend the significance of this, I must take you on a journey back to the roots of my story and how it all began.

I was born and grew up mostly in Manchester and if you haven't heard of it, just imagine clouds, rain, and the occasional day of sunshine, as if the Universe accidentally left the window open.

I lived in a place called Wythenshawe that, at the time, was known to be the largest council estate in Britain. One house, four kids, two parents (sometimes), and a lot of noise. I mean, a *lot* of noise.

My childhood could be summed up as a lively mix of *Coronation Street* meets *The Hunger Games*. Communication in our house? Oh, that was simple: he who shouted the loudest got heard. It wasn't so much a conversation as a competition for survival of the vocal cords.

I was the eldest girl, sandwiched between an older brother who preferred silence and two younger sisters who could scream at a pitch so high, even dolphins would wince. As for my parents, well, their simultaneous presence at home was as rare as a solar eclipse and just as unpredictable. When they *did* happen to be in the same room, the air was instantly charged. Arguments weren't just common, they were like clockwork. It felt less like a home and more like living inside a thunderstorm, where every clash of words was followed by a downpour of emotions, and lightning bolts of anger would light up the room.

Dad, bless him, worked long shifts, probably out of self-preservation more than anything. I used to think "Wow, what a hard worker!" But now I'm pretty sure he just fancied some peace and quiet away from our circus of a household. Can't say I blame him.

We moved house more times than I could count, usually with as much planning as you'd put into making a sandwich. One minute we were settled (sort of), the next we were packing boxes. It was like living on a Monopoly board where every roll of the dice landed on 'Go to Jail' except, you know, instead of jail it was a new school, new neighbourhood, new everything.

School was a different brand of torture. By the time I was nine, I'd perfected the art of becoming invisible, at least in my head. I'd sit at my desk, daydreaming that I could just *disappear*. Who knew invisibility would be the superpower of choice for a shy kid? I didn't fit in, but I had my imagination and let me tell you, it was *wild*. I could go from being a ballerina to a world-famous singer to a spy, all before the lunch bell rang.

Home, though? Oh, that was a different story. At home, I didn't *want* to be invisible, I wanted to be seen! But there was always something louder, more dramatic, or more tear-filled happening that kept me in the background. It was like living in a soap opera, except I didn't even get a decent storyline.

My sisters? Absolute drama queens. They had screaming and shouting to get attention down to a fine art. Me? I was told I was old enough to "look after myself." At nine. Which, by the way, was Mum code for "You're not getting any attention."

I felt lost and alone in my own world, so I continued plodding on, hiding in the crowd, feeling anxious most of the time and always trying to blend in at school. Hiding at break times in the toilets or a corner in the playground.

Until one day in the classroom, I got noticed and picked out of the crowd. This was a new experience for me and after it, one I was determined never to repeat.

It was reading day in our class, the teacher asked, "Who would like to read out loud to the class?" If no one volunteered, she would choose someone to go to the front of the class and read. Throughout most of the term, the children who loved the attention (and could read!) would eagerly put their hands up. I would then relax, breathe and get back to my daydreaming. But not today.

I remember it was a bright, warm, spring day, the sun was streaming through the large windows lighting up the classroom. Me in my usual safe place at the back of the classroom, head down on the wooden desk, enjoying the warmth of the sun on the side of my face, feeling invisible – or at least I thought I was!

I can only imagine that it must have been the sunlight that day that had exposed me because my name got called out by the teacher. I remember thinking *how the hell did she even see me?* I was so far back, and I thought I was so invisible and tucked away.

At first, I ignored her and kept my head down, but my name was called again, and I felt a sudden tidal wave of emotions that started to run through my body. I remember wishing the fire alarm would go off, but it didn't!

I slowly got up from my desk, legs feeling like jelly, palms of my hands clammy. Tightly clutching my book as if my life depended on it, I made my way to the front of the class. Eventually arriving at the front, I turned, and a sea of faces stared back at me. From the corner of my eye, I saw two boys giggling and laughing at me.

The teacher looked at me and asked me to read the page out loud to the class. My throat was so dry, my mouth felt like sandpaper, hands visibly shaking as I clasped the book tightly. I felt my face start to burn, and it felt like I was overheating and being consumed by fire. My heart started to beat so fast I could feel the speed and energy transfer into the shaking of my hands. All I wanted to do was run away, but I was stuck, stuck in front of a class that could now see me.

I was so exposed and embarrassed, I felt naked. Opening my mouth, I began to read, racing through the words on the page as fast as I possibly could, without pausing or stopping for a breath.

"There, I've done it!" I exclaimed and quickly ran back to the safety of my desk. Everyone in the class reacted by bursting into laughter at my erratic behaviour. With my face still ablaze and on fire, I hurriedly took cover, head down, wishing I could just disappear. That day I made up my mind I would never be visible or feel exposed again.

Avoidance became my new behaviour; it worked well. Going forward I created illnesses to avoid going to school and that rewarded me with the attention and the love I so craved from my mum. All this without needing to shout the loudest; I felt a release of tension from the inside and happiness and contentment took its place. Pretending to be ill and this way of acting had achieved my perfect way of feeling and being.

I had baffled the medical profession with 'imaginary' pains in my legs and feet. Of course, these pains meant I couldn't walk to school, and I'd even convinced myself that these pains were real. My lie had become my truth.

Looking back now, it's a little embarrassing to admit how many unnecessary tests and investigations I went through, all because of my "mystery illness". Doctors were scratching their heads, running test after test, looking for the elusive cause. Meanwhile, there I was – nine years old and living my best life in A&E, fascinated by the bustling wards, watching nurses magically melt away patients' pain. I was convinced I was at the centre of it all, the main character in this hospital drama. It felt like an adventure!

Whilst I sat there watching all this unfold, spending what I thought to be quality time with my mum, we grew closer. In the busy hospital corridors, my mum shared stories of herself being a nurse and a particular story of when she was still in nurse training and had found out she was pregnant with me. She reminisced about walking the same corridors where we were waiting that afternoon, noting that they hadn't changed – they still looked the same as when she was training in the NHS.

She continued with her story, telling me that whilst still in nurse training, and feeling so happy in her nurse's uniform, she had made a wish. She wished that the baby she was carrying would grow up and want to be a nurse just like her and live her dream – the dream she wouldn't get to complete because, back then, there was very little childcare support so my mum wouldn't be able to continue in her dream job of becoming a nurse.

I'm sure this message or wish must have somehow been encoded and transferred into my DNA because I certainly felt at home in the hospital environment, it was so real and exciting, I felt so alive, and it smelt divine. It became very addictive for me to be there. I couldn't imagine anywhere else I would want to be or spend my time. I decided there and then that, when I was old enough, I would become a nurse and heal people's pain. That pain they all must feel deep inside just like I did.

The meeting of my best friend

It was around this time, aged nine, that I met my first real friend.

We'd moved again, this time with about as much planning as a last-minute pizza order. On our first day in the new house, I met Lynn, who showed up at my door looking just as shocked as I was. Turns out, she was expecting her friend to open the door, the same friend who had crashed at Lynn's house the night before and was supposed to be back home bright and early.

What Lynn didn't know was that her friend's family had pulled a vanishing act, secretly swapping houses with us in the dead of night to dodge debt collectors. So, there we were, my family, starting a whole new chapter with zero warning and barely a chair to sit on!

After a short and confusing conversation between us both, Lynn and I found common ground, and she asked if I would like to go out and play. From that day, she became my new best friend.

Meeting Lynn was a game-changer in my childhood, shifting me from isolation to companionship. Over the following months, I found out more about Lynn's life. Her mum had died of cancer four years earlier. Growing up and losing her mum at the most memorable time, Christmas Eve, tainted Lynn's childhood with bittersweet memories, and she often struggled at that time of year. Lynn always feared getting cancer herself and would always ask, "Do you think I will get cancer?" I always reassured her, saying only old people die or get cancer, we are kids, you'll be fine.

Lynn's dad had recently re-married, and she had a stepmom and four older stepsisters. Lynn struggled with this family change and constantly wished she could escape from her new family dynamics and home life.

I understood why she wanted to escape, which was highlighted one Sunday afternoon when tears rolled down her face. She sat close to me on the playground and started telling me all about her home life. She cried endless tears as she told me how she hated her life, living in a house she no longer felt was her home, feeling pushed out and bullied by her stepmother and step-siblings to the extent that she was being treated like a real-life Cinderella.

I deeply empathised, picking up her deep feelings and being so deeply moved by Lynn's upset, and taking these feelings on board as if they were my own. I wanted to heal her pain, to rescue her. I suggested she should come and spend more time with me, as much as she could, and she did exactly that. Over time, Lynn became happier knowing she could call and spend time at my house, a safe but chaotic place, in between all the housework duties she had been given by her stepmom and sisters.

Lynn was two years older than me and very smart, and over the following years our friendship grew deeper. We became inseparable, more like sisters than friends. Practically living at our house, my mum and dad didn't seem to mind. She was even invited on our family holidays, often helping my mum with babysitting and taking care of my two younger sisters. I remember my mum always giving her praise for her beautiful handwriting and wonderful spelling. Frequently hearing this, I would often get jealous but then laugh it off. I didn't care, I told myself, Lynn deserved the praise more than I did, she was the clever one and after all, she was the one who went to school every day. Whereas I had continued to create illness throughout term times until the long summer holidays arrived (when I would suddenly make a full recovery from the pains in my legs). I'd then enjoy the long warm summer days, out roaming the fields with Lynn, my best and loyal friend. We were always looking for excitement and adventure to fill our days, enjoying our freedom from dawn until dusk.

Looking back, it's almost funny how we balanced each other out. I provided the chaos, she provided the brains. Together, we made quite the duo.

By the start of senior school, I knew I needed to change tactics. Faking illnesses had run its course, and it was becoming way too obvious. I'd created a pattern: always sick before school, but magically better during holidays. It was time for a new game plan.

At least things had settled at home. My parents had finally stopped bouncing between houses, and for the first time in a while, the place we were living in felt like home. My focus started to shift. I felt more confident, happier in myself, and ready to take a fresh approach.

That's when I came up with my latest idea. Each morning, I'd go through the usual routine, get dressed in my school uniform, pack a change of clothes in my bag, and head out the door like the responsible student I was pretending to be.

But instead of going to school, I'd meet up with Lynn.

By now, Lynn had grown into a teenager who, like me, was hungry for excitement and desperate for an escape from the long, boring school days. We were partners in crime, both looking for a taste of freedom. So, instead of marching off to our classes, we'd hop on the bus into the city centre.

It felt *amazing* to be free. With our combined dinner money, we could just about afford bus fare. We even started smoking, convinced it made us look cool and sophisticated. Most days, we'd claim our spots at the top of the double-decker bus, puffing away on cigarettes, reapplying our makeup, and combing our hair as we cruised into Manchester. The city felt like our playground, full of endless possibilities.

We spent our days exploring the bustling city centre, feeling oh-so-grown-up and rebellious. Every day was a new adventure, a fresh taste of freedom. It was the late 1970s, and Manchester was bursting with energy. The punk scene had exploded, and the streets were alive with colour – electric pinks, neon greens, and jet-black Mohawks everywhere you looked. Groups of older kids strutted through the city, proudly showing off their multi-coloured hair, nose rings, and clothes held together with oversized safety pins.

For the first time in my life, I *wanted* to be seen. Arcades and underground markets became our playgrounds, filled with noise, neon lights, and that perfect mix of excitement and danger. I soaked up every ounce of the city's vibrant energy, watching the punks like they were rock stars. Lynn and I would follow them as if by walking in their footsteps, we might catch some of that cool, rebellious magic.

But by the time I turned fourteen, the party ended abruptly. My days of dodging school caught up with me. My parents, who had been blissfully unaware of my *academic truancy,* were suddenly thrust into the spotlight when they were summoned to court over my not-so-impressive attendance record. To say they were furious is an understatement. They had no idea I'd been skipping school for months, and honestly, I'd become such a pro at it that even *I* half-believed I was still a student.

Meanwhile, Lynn had changed. She had left school, landed a job in an office, and in what felt like a blink, became someone new. She'd found her confidence – and a whole new group of friends. They were older, had money, and could do things I couldn't afford, or honestly, wasn't even interested in. Suddenly, it felt like Lynn was slipping away from me, and I was left behind, stranded in the world of school uniforms and empty bus rides.

That was the first time I truly experienced loss. It felt like I'd been abandoned, like a vital piece of me had been ripped away. I couldn't make sense of it, but I knew it hurt deeply. The tears I cried then were real, unlike the crocodile tears I used to fake being sick. When I finally stopped crying, I decided. I wasn't going to speak to her again. Not ever. If she wanted to leave me behind, then fine. I would disappear from her life just as quickly as she had from mine.

Time passed and, eventually, it was my turn to leave school. I'll never forget the day my final school report came in the post. I opened the envelope, expecting...well, *something*, but it was practically blank. My name was at the top, and the only other thing inside was a comment from my form teacher: *"Who is this girl?"* I laughed. It didn't matter. I had succeeded in my mission. I had remained invisible, hiding from the bullying girls, slipping under the radar, and disappearing from school life without anyone even noticing I was gone.

But reality has a funny way of catching up with you. A few months later, it hit me like a ton of bricks: I was leaving school with no qualifications, no real education, and no plan. The question burned in my mind: how on earth was I going to become a nurse? I couldn't even spell 'Wythenshawe', the area I lived in, let alone handle medical jargon.

As I sat there, trying to figure out my future, hoping for some divine intervention, my mum broke the silence. "You have to be realistic, Jackie," she said gently. "To be a nurse, you need a good education, and you've hardly had any."

She didn't need to tell me that, I already knew. My inner critic had been yelling at me for days, reminding me of everything I couldn't do. And there I was, standing on the edge of the big, wide world, feeling lost and wondering what on earth I was going to do with the rest of my life.

Takeaway Lesson

Avoidance had been my escape route for years – a sneaky little trick that worked well in the short term. Faking illness gave me the love and attention I desperately craved from my mum. It was a strategy that relieved the inner tension I carried, swapping my anxiety for a fleeting sense of happiness. I became so good at lying, even I believed the imaginary pains were real, baffling the doctors with my performance.

But here's what I eventually learned: while avoidance might feel like a quick fix, it's no long-term solution. You can't lie your way to happiness or convince yourself that pretending problems don't exist will make them disappear. Sooner or later, reality catches up with you.

And when we avoid the real issues, we blur the lines between what's real and what we're running from. Eventually, it all comes crashing down.

So, here's my question: What are you avoiding in your life?

Chapter Two
The Determination Years

Have you ever wanted something so badly that nothing, not even your own doubts, could stop you? That was me. Every time I thought about becoming a nurse, I felt electric, like I was finally alive. It became my mission, my obsession. I decided right then and there, I would fight for this dream until the bitter end. If I could just get into college, I'd have my chance.

Making that decision was the moment everything shifted. I knew I had to stop hiding. The inner voice that usually whispered "You're not clever enough" or "People will laugh at you" tried its best to hold me back, reminding me of all the old school anxieties. But this time was different. This time, I had to push through. The fear was still there, but my desire to be a nurse was stronger.

So, I pushed through the fear and self-doubt. And somehow, against all odds, I got myself onto a college course. It took three years of hard work – three long years of fighting against that voice in my head telling me I wasn't good enough – but I did it. I got the qualifications I needed to start my journey as a nurse. And with every little victory, I was climbing that ladder toward my goal.

Now, don't get me wrong, it wasn't easy. Every exam felt like a hurdle, and even when I passed, I brushed it off as luck. My family barely noticed. Looking back, I realise I never celebrated any of my milestones, and neither did they. I stayed invisible, as if all my hard work didn't even exist.

All I wanted was a simple "Well done" from my mum. Just some recognition, some praise. I longed for that hug that never came. But instead of letting it defeat me, I used that emptiness as fuel. I told myself, "One day they'll notice." So, I kept going, racking up certificates and qualifications like they were trophies in a game. But no matter how much I achieved, the praise never came.

Nursing became more than a job, it became my identity, my purpose. I wasn't just patching up cuts or taking care of patients, I was helping people heal their emotional pain. In some strange way, nursing gave me a release from my own inner turmoil. By connecting with my patients, hearing their stories, and seeing their resilience, I started working through my own pain, bit by bit, hoping to find my own cure.

But let's rewind to my early days in college, when life was a wild mix of studying, partying, and surviving endless shifts at the local hospital. I was a trainee nursing assistant by day and a party girl by night. Every weekend, I craved excitement – going out, getting drunk, living life to the fullest.

It was during this time that I had my first serious relationship with a man named Kevin. I was 17; he was 24, a popular DJ at the local pub. He was *the* guy everyone knew and liked, with his soft-spoken, caring nature. I'd spend most weekends at the pub, downing drinks with my friends, hanging out by the dance floor, and mustering up the courage (thanks, alcohol) to ask Kevin to play my favourite songs. I was obsessed with Luther Vandross, Boy George, and my ultimate favourite, Patrice Rushen's *Forget Me Nots*. I'd flutter my lashes and pretend I was cool while practising my very awkward flirting techniques.

Kevin was a good guy – too good. He cheered me on, made me feel confident, and was always there for me. But after a year, I got bored. He was too nice, too predictable, and let's be honest, he was getting a bit too serious for my liking. So, I ended it with the classic line, "We can still be friends." Of course, Kevin didn't take it well. He kept calling, showing up at the pub, buying me drinks, playing my songs, and helping me home when I'd had one too many (which was often). He was like my personal bank manager and taxi service. And while I felt a bit guilty for stringing him along, I knew deep down I had moved on.

Around this time, Lynn – my ex-best friend – reappeared in my life. Out of nowhere, she contacted me, saying she missed me. She was getting married and wanted me at her wedding. My first instinct was to tell her to get lost, but curiosity got the better of me. I agreed to go.

Surprisingly, reconnecting with Lynn felt like no time had passed. It wasn't the same old friendship; it was deeper. We picked up right where we left off, like she was the missing piece of me that had returned. It was a relief. After her wedding, we stayed in touch, and I was there for the birth of her first baby boy. But two years later, at 23, it was my turn to leave Lynn behind.

The Universe had other plans for me. Out of the blue, an opportunity appeared to leave Manchester and do further nurse training in Newcastle. It was terrifying, but I knew this was my chance. My future as a nurse depended on it.

When I told my family, it was like I'd kicked a hornet's nest. Panic spread through them. Suddenly, I was no longer invisible. They begged me not to go, their fear practically tangible. "What if you never come back?" they asked, desperate to keep me close. But deep down, I knew this was my moment. For the first time, I was putting myself first. So, I packed my bags and left for Newcastle, stepping into the unknown to chase my dreams.

It was the boldest decision I'd ever made. And while it was scary, I knew it was the only way to discover who I truly was. That journey would change me forever.

Takeaway Lesson

Determination isn't about the absence of fear – it's about pushing through it. It's facing the doubts in your head and choosing to believe in yourself anyway. The journey ahead might seem overwhelming, but it's those moments of courage that lead to real growth. By stepping into the unknown, we give ourselves the chance to see just how much we're truly capable of.

Chapter Three
The Newcastle Years

I arrived in Newcastle in the early spring of March 1987 to continue my nursing career journey. Back in the 1980s, nurses trained in the NHS on the wards, gaining valuable hands-on experiences. I lived across the road from the hospital, in nurses' accommodation, so I didn't have far to travel. The training was strict, almost like being in the army. Uniforms and hats needed to be meticulously starched and the appropriate black, blue, and red pens had to be on display in top pockets.

This was a very proud National Health Service (NHS) and a very status-conscious environment where nurses were ranked by the number of stripes on their hats, indicating their level of ability and years in service.

The doctors were worshipped like gods and only the highest level of nurse would be allowed to go on the ward rounds and present the patients. At the time, observing this play out on the wards, it tapped into my feelings of anxiety and vulnerability, and brought out feelings of never being good enough. I wanted to hide myself and my lack of stripes, but I stayed visible, striving away, determined to gain my stripes and build myself up to be seen throughout my training ranks. Every day, I had to try and stop my hands shaking whilst I carried cups of tea on saucers made for the gods. (That's what we called the doctors who would sit in their offices looking very poker-faced and serious about life.)

But there was a silver lining to my move to Newcastle, and her name was Annie. She was from Hartlepool, just up the road from Newcastle, and had enrolled on the same nursing course and, lucky for me, moved into the same nurses' accommodation. We hit it off right away. On our very first meeting, she knocked on my door, introduced herself, and within minutes, we were bonding over cups of tea and tragic life stories.

That night she told me the story of her best friend, Janet, who had been tragically murdered by a crazed ex-wife in the local town shop. It was a tale straight out of a horror film, and as she recounted it, I sat there, wide-eyed, wondering what kind of place I had just moved to. Was Newcastle safe? Should I start wearing a stab vest under my nursing uniform?

I made another cup of tea and was intrigued to find out more as Annie continued telling me about her best friend, who had been threatened many times by the boyfriend's ex-wife. The ex-wife would constantly call into the shop where she worked, shouting and threatening that she was going to kill her.

A few months later that threat was carried out with a vicious knife attack. It took place in the shop, one busy lunchtime, with plenty of people to witness the attack. Annie's friend had been stabbed eighteen times and left in a pool of blood on the floor that day she lost her life, causing a ripple effect for the loved ones left behind. Life would never be the same again for her family and best friend.

Not long after the attack, the ex-wife was arrested and remains behind bars to this day, being one of the longest-serving women prisoners.

Wow, I remember thinking at the time, I know I've come here from a large, rough, council estate, but I'd never heard of anyone where I lived that had actually been murdered!

Annie leaned in closer, her voice full of emotion as she finished telling me about her friend, Janet. She looked at me with wide eyes, convinced that our meeting wasn't just some random chance. "I mean, your name starts with a 'J', just like Janet's," she said, "and you even share the same birthday! You both would've been the same age."

To Annie, this wasn't just a coincidence; it was a sign from the Universe. She truly believed we were meant to meet, that I had been sent to help her through the grief and loss she was still carrying. As she spoke, I could feel the sincerity in her words, and strangely, it started to make sense to me too.

It hit me then: helping people heal wasn't just something I did, it was part of who I was. In that moment, sitting there with Annie, I realised I was exactly where I was supposed to be.

From that first meeting, we became best friends. That evening, we decided to take a stroll, eager to explore our new surroundings. As we wandered through the unfamiliar streets, a sense of peace washed over me, something I had never truly felt before. The world seemed to slow down, and for the first time in my life, I felt utterly relaxed, as if I had finally found where I belonged.

That night, as I returned to my small, unfamiliar room in the nursing accommodation, the reality of my new life began to sink in. I lay awake in the narrow single bed, my mind racing with a whirlwind of thoughts. The room was dimly lit by the soft glow of the moon outside my window, casting eerie shadows that only added to my restlessness. I gazed out at the clear night sky, the vastness of it mirroring the uncertainty I felt within. A hundred thoughts tumbled through my mind – thoughts about the bold move I had just made, the adventure I had embarked upon, and the new life that lay ahead of me. The feeling was a potent mix of excitement and fear, like standing on the edge of a cliff, ready to leap into the unknown.

Over the next two years, Annie and I spent time studying and working long shifts. On our nights off, we went out partying, making memories that would last forever. I often reflect on those years with fond memories of lots of laughter and happiness. They were happy times when I was on my way to becoming me and obtaining my dream goal, moving up the ranks to be a registered nurse, and achieving more stripes on my hat – the most important focus in my life at the time.

It wasn't long into our training that we both met boyfriends. After a short six-month relationship, Annie got engaged and started planning her wedding and moving on.

Swept along with the idea and excitement of engagements and getting married, I didn't want to be left alone after she got married, so I decided to do the same with my boyfriend, Paul, who on the surface, seemed perfect. He became my fiancé. But deep down, I couldn't shake the feeling that I wanted to be free, like I was forcing myself into a role I wasn't ready for. Looking back, I can see how I was allowing myself to slip into following other people's choices, I was anxious and in fear of being left on the shelf, lost and alone.

Everybody liked Paul, and friends often commented how we looked like the perfect couple. When I first met Paul, he overwhelmed me with the love and attention he constantly showed me. Over time, I got used to it and it made me feel safe and secure. We went everywhere together, he even walked me to and from work. He could not do enough for me.

A short time after getting engaged, I moved out of the nurse accommodation and into Paul's two-bedroom house to set up home together. Life was settled in both work and home. It felt balanced and we were happy.

As the months passed, I found myself increasingly overwhelmed by the wedding arrangements that needed to be made. Paul's parents were relentless, calling every week to push for setting the date, eager to get the ball rolling. Their excitement was palpable – they were financially secure and saw this wedding as the grand event of the year, a project they could throw themselves into with no expense spared. They made it clear they were happy to cover all the costs, ensuring the wedding would be nothing short of spectacular.

But what was meant to be a gesture of generosity quickly became a source of tension. My dad, a proud man who had always taken care of his family, was determined to foot the bill himself. He was willing to go into debt if it meant he could uphold his sense of responsibility and pride. The situation spiralled into a bitter clash between the two sets of parents, each determined to assert their own vision for the wedding. What should have been a joyous time became a battlefield, with me caught in the crossfire.

As the tension mounted, I felt myself shrinking away from the conflict. The constant tug-of-war over control made me feel invisible, as if my own desires for the wedding were irrelevant. The focus had shifted entirely from what Paul and I wanted to what our parents wanted to prove to each other. I felt like a pawn in their game, my voice drowned out by the noise of their arguments.

In response, I began to withdraw, retreating into myself as a means of self-preservation. I stopped engaging in conversations about the wedding and avoided any discussion of dates or plans. I felt powerless, and delaying the wedding became my only form of control. The more I withdrew, the more invisible I became, not just to my parents and Paul's parents, but to myself. It was as though I had disappeared into the background of my own life, letting the decisions and chaos swirl around me without daring to take a stand.

The very idea of setting a date or moving forward with the planning became something I dreaded, a task I couldn't bear to face. My withdrawal wasn't just from the wedding plans – it was from the expectations, the pressure, and the growing realisation that I was losing sight of what truly mattered to me. In my efforts to avoid the conflict, I had also avoided confronting my own needs and desires, leaving me feeling more lost and disconnected than ever.

It was just as well that I delayed the wedding plans because, after twelve months of living with Paul, the cracks in our relationship began to surface. At first, they were subtle – small clues that something wasn't quite right, a nagging feeling that things were beginning to change. But as time went on, these clues became impossible to ignore.

I started to notice a troubling pattern in Paul's behaviour, especially when it came to my social life. Whenever I made plans to go out with friends, his mood would shift dramatically. What started as minor irritations would quickly escalate into full-blown arguments, always just before I was about to leave. It was as if he couldn't stand the idea of me enjoying time with others, away from his influence. Each time, Paul would pick at me, finding faults where there were none until I was left feeling upset and guilty – convinced that I was somehow the cause of the conflict.

Every time I returned home from a night out with friends, Paul would insist on a meticulous debrief, demanding an hour-by-hour account of my movements. He would bombard me with questions: "Did you talk to anyone? Did your friends talk to any men? How long did you stay at each pub or club?" His interrogation was relentless and exhausting.

At a time when there were no mobile phones to check in or track locations, these debriefs became his way of controlling my life, ensuring that I felt guilty and anxious even after a simple evening out. What should have been harmless conversations often spiralled into arguments, leaving me wide awake, unable to sleep despite my exhaustion.

As the stress of these confrontations mounted, I found myself retreating from my social life, going out less and less just to avoid the inevitable tension. It wasn't worth the peace I lost every time I walked back through that door. But as I pulled back from my friends, I began to notice other disturbing patterns in Paul's behaviour.

On weekends, he played football, but it was never just a game for him. Arguments on the pitch often escalated into physical fights, leaving him with broken fingers that required bandaging or splints. These injuries became so frequent that they were almost routine. Yet, Paul seemed to revel in the violence, boasting about how he had used his fists to "solve" disputes. Being sent off the field became part of the thrill for him, just as much as the broken bones were badges of honour.

When the A&E department finally warned Paul that if he kept breaking his knuckles and fingers, he would face long-term damage and possibly require surgery, he simply laughed it off, recounting the incidents as if they were just part of the game. His nonchalance about the potential consequences of his actions was chilling, but at the time, I didn't fully grasp the implications.

I didn't connect the dots – or maybe I chose not to – until one night later that year when an evening out shifted everything. Suddenly, the patterns I had ignored for so long became painfully clear, and I could no longer deny the truth about who Paul really was.

Pattern becoming clear to see – sometimes we don't want the truth to be true

It was my favourite time of year: early autumn, cold and fresh with leaves starting to fall. My birthday month of October had arrived, and sadly I will always remember this birthday for all the wrong reasons: the evening that changed my life.

A few months before my birthday, I had met a nurse colleague called Jo from Scotland, we had briefly been on the same training course, and we had developed a strong bond working together on the wards. After Jo had completed her training, she moved back home to Scotland, promising to keep in touch and come back to Newcastle and visit me.

My birthday weekend was the ideal time for Jo to come and stay to celebrate my birthday. Living in a small house near the town centre and train station, it was easy for her to come to stay the weekend, and to celebrate and enjoy my birthday.

I was so excited and looking forward to seeing her again, however, Paul didn't seem very happy about it, telling me he would be working most of that weekend when she was coming to visit. Which, to be honest, I felt secretly pleased about. I had not had a good night out with friends for months and this felt like the perfect birthday present to give myself.

It was early lunchtime when Jo arrived at the house that Friday, we started chatting away, catching up, and opened a bottle of wine. The drinks were flowing with ease, just like the conversation. Time moved on as if in the bat of an eyelid. By late afternoon, we decided to go out for a late lunch.

Arriving in Newcastle town centre on a busy Friday afternoon, we soon forgot about ordering any food. Jo liked a drink and so did I, so we were out, out in the town drinking for the full day. Moving from bar to bar.

The day rapidly turned into night and as the night started unfolding, Jo met a guy. They were getting on very well and she signalled to me she liked him. Feeling very drunk I decided it was time for me to go home, I called a taxi and told Jo to stay at the club and follow me home when she was ready.

I waited outside the club until the taxi picked me up and within ten minutes I had arrived outside my house. I managed to stay upright as I placed the key into position to open the front door. Once inside the hallway, I set my eyes to focus on and follow the light coming from the bottom of the living room door at the end of the hallway. Inside, my fiancé Paul sat drinking cans of beer and watching football.

On entering the room Paul got up and suddenly started shouting at me, "Where the fuck have you been all day?" He moved towards the wastepaper basket in the corner of the room and pushed it over so that the empty bottles of wine and beer cans came tumbling out onto the carpet. "Pick them up," he said.

I drunkenly laughed at him.

He pushed past me and went into the kitchen, returning seconds later with the largest kitchen knife we owned. I froze as he dragged me by my hair to the basket that now lay empty. He was standing over me, the knife waving in his hand, repeating for me to pick up the empty wine bottles and beer cans.

I had suddenly sobered up. He was deadly serious. I started to pick up the bottles and cans, my life flashing before me, as he continued to shout abuse into my face about his disgust at my drunken behaviour. I had visions flash before me of being murdered there and then on my birthday, or ending up in intensive care slashed to pieces, so I didn't answer back, I would just do as I was told and hopefully, I would be safe and survive. After what seemed like hours, probably in reality a few minutes, he put the knife down on the arm of the sofa. His mood suddenly switched as fast as changing a TV channel.

"Right," he said, "are we going to bed now?"

I couldn't believe the sudden change in him, and I managed to voice my reply, "Yes, I just need to tidy up." Then I told him to go ahead and he went upstairs.

My mind was racing, I needed to escape. I grabbed my coat and bag and then left the house. Halfway down the road, I managed to flag down a taxi and I arrived back at the club where I had left Jo. She couldn't believe what had happened and how shaken I looked.

That night we managed to find a cheap hotel and sat up talking until the early hours, trying to unravel and make sense of the events of the last few hours and the threat of nearly losing my life.

The clarity was both a relief and a burden, a painful awakening to the reality that the person I had been living with was driven by deep-seated narcissistic tendencies. Confronting this truth was like waking up from a long, disorienting dream – it was clear, harsh, and difficult to accept. The realisation forced me to grapple with the uncomfortable truth that the love I had invested in the relationship had been overshadowed by manipulation and control, and it was a truth I could no longer ignore or rationalise away.

Still in shock the following day, I made plans and arranged to move into a temporary room back in the nursing accommodation. Two porters I had known since arriving and working in the hospital offered to help me move my stuff from the house. That following morning whilst Paul was still at work, I packed all my belongings and left the house, putting the key through the letter box as the door closed for the final time.

A couple of months had slipped by, and I found myself back in the seeming safety of the nurses' accommodation. My room was small but functional, with a communal kitchen that met my needs.

January had cast a shadow over everything – the days were dark and dismal, quickly giving way to long, gloomy nights. This environment made it all too easy to blend into the background, to become invisible once again.

But the shadows outside mirrored the fears inside me. My mind spun tales of how Paul might somehow track me down, and paranoia began to gnaw at me. I found myself jumping at every unexpected sound, hiding behind corners, and sending friends on errands to the local shops to avoid going out myself.

The constant stress and exhaustion left me feeling frayed and on edge.

Desperate for relief, I decided it was time to visit my GP, hoping for something, anything, that would help me sleep better.

The next day, I walked into the clinic, seeking solace in a prescription for sleeping tablets. As the GP began updating my medical history, I felt my focus slipping. My thoughts were consumed by a singular wish for a simple solution to my sleepless nights. Then, the GP's question snapped me back to the present moment: "When was your last period?"

I was struck dumb, unable to recall even the most basic details. "Could you be pregnant?" he asked, his voice tinged with concern. I was taken aback, my mind scrambling to grasp the possibility. Pregnant? No, I thought. It couldn't be – I hadn't considered it at all.

The GP, sensing my confusion, asked me to provide a urine sample right there and then. I moved through the process mechanically, my thoughts still reeling from the sudden turn of events. Five minutes later, I was back in his office, my heart pounding in my chest as he peered over his glasses at the test strip in front of him. His eyes met mine with a look of solemnity, and then he spoke words that seemed to hang in the air like a heavy fog: "It's positive. You're pregnant."

The weight of his words hit me with the force of a tidal wave. Pregnant. The realisation crashed over me, and I sat there, stunned, as the reality of the situation settled in. The small room, the hidden life, the endless paranoia – it all felt distant now, eclipsed by the enormity of this new truth. I was pregnant, and nothing would ever be the same again.

My mind raced as I replayed the last few months in agonising detail. I had been drowning my worries in alcohol, chain-smoking cigarettes, and had even undergone a general anaesthetic for wisdom teeth removal – all of which were dangerously risky during the early stages of pregnancy. Yet here I was, pregnant and completely unprepared. The gravity of the situation hit me like a sledgehammer: I was nine weeks pregnant, working on a hectic orthopaedic ward as part of my training, and the thought of raising a baby alone felt like the end of my world.

The next day, I made the difficult decision to confide in the nurse matron. Her response was blunt and unsettling. She told me that having the baby would be throwing away my career, and she offered to arrange a termination for the following week. That evening, and every evening that followed, I was consumed by a torrent of thoughts. Alone in my small room, I wrestled with the monumental decision ahead of me.

Would Paul ever find out about the pregnancy?

Did I even want him to be part of this child's life?

The questions swirled around my mind, relentless and unanswered, leaving me isolated with my fears and uncertainties, without any outside distractions to offer respite.

This was the first time I turned inward, seeking guidance from my deepest self. A powerful, unwavering sense emerged from within, urging me to prioritise the life growing inside me, to embrace the challenge and choose to have the baby. It felt like a call to return to Manchester, a place where I believed I would find safety and support. Yet, even as this inner conviction took hold, doubt lingered, whispering questions of uncertainty – was this truly the right path, or was I simply grasping at hope?

Takeaway Lesson

The true gifts in life often emerge from the most difficult decisions we face. What once seemed like insurmountable challenges and life-altering choices eventually revealed themselves as profound blessings. While starting over is never easy, especially when it involves letting go of a love that has turned into fear, the strength and clarity I discovered in those moments of uncertainty became invaluable.

The decision to walk away and forge a new path, though daunting, marked a pivotal moment of growth. It was a testament to my inner resilience and a step toward an uncertain future, guided by newfound strength and self-trust. Embracing the unknown, I learned that sometimes the hardest choices lead to the most transformative and empowering experiences.

Chapter Four
Going Backwards to Come Forward

Within a month of making my mind up to leave Newcastle, I was back living in Manchester, back at my parents' home.

Feeling very controlled, I felt lost and overwhelmed. Like I'd slipped back in time, I had taken my place back within the family fold, moving uncomfortably into the familiar drama and chaos I once knew and grew up in. I needed to move on from this familiar chaos I had outgrown, I could now see how different I had become living away for so long. I had changed.

I put my name forward for a small council flat and waited patiently for one to be offered, hoping it would be before my baby was born. It was time for me to find my own place, make my own life and live the way I wanted to. I needed to create a calm space for the new arrival growing fast inside me.

My decision to continue with the pregnancy still felt right. I just didn't know how I would provide financially and give this baby the best life it deserved.

In June 1990, I gave birth to a beautiful baby boy. I called him Ben. It was bittersweet on the ward, watching other mums be greeted with flowers, cards and happy tears while my tears were from feeling sorry for myself and being all alone without the other person who had been part of making this wonderful human being.

The first time I held Ben all my worries and doubts melted away, he melted my heart. New, unfamiliar feelings of love, joy and protection flowed through me, I became a fine-tuned radar picking up on every cry or move he made. My intuition became very strong, stronger than ever before and I enjoyed the inner connection and allowed it to guide me. One thing was certain, I would provide the best life for him. I felt a tremendous strength, powerful determination inside me that became activated like a lioness protecting her cub. He would be my focus from that moment on.

The Move

Later that year, I was offered and moved into a small bottom-floor two-bedroomed council flat and set up home, just in time for the new year and new start. Ben was now six months old and ready to move to his new home.

On moving day, January's cold and crisp air greeted me as I stepped into the empty flat. Despite the chill outside, the moment I walked in, I felt a warm, welcoming energy. It was as though the space itself was inviting me to be happy there. This simple, reassuring feeling was all I needed to know that this new place was meant for me.

Becoming a mother brought a wave of new emotions and insights. My inner senses seemed to sharpen, offering me a deeper sense of guidance and safety. Adjusting to these feelings was challenging, but they brought a comforting sense of contentment and trust in my own intuition.

Over the next two years, my dad became an invaluable support. We grew much closer as he frequently stayed over at my flat to look after my son while I worked part-time at the local hospital. This arrangement worked perfectly: my dad would babysit during my night shifts and then head to his job as a porter at the same hospital early the next morning. It saved me a significant amount on childcare costs and allowed me to maintain a career and interact with adults.

As time went on, something unusual happened in the flat. The presence I first felt seemed to interact more actively with our environment. For example, lights would turn on by themselves when my son cried, and his lullaby lamp would start playing at night on its own. These occurrences didn't scare me; they felt like a reassuring presence, blending seamlessly with the energy of our home. Although I didn't share these experiences with anyone, fearing they might think I was crazy or suffering from postnatal depression, I felt confident that this presence was there to protect us.

Then one night a friend came over and I decided to share these experiences with him. His reaction was dismissive and mocking – he didn't believe me and even laughed, asking me to prove it. Determined to show him, I agreed to test my connection with the energy in the flat. I asked him for an item to hold and he handed me his wallet. Closing my eyes, I held the wallet in my hands. At that moment, the lights flickered, and the TV turned off by itself. My friend's reaction changed from disbelief to alarm.

As I continued to focus and trust my inner guidance, I felt a warm, brilliant energy envelop me, as if a light had been switched on inside me. With my eyes still closed, I could visualise a man's presence beside me. When I opened my eyes, I described this man's physical appearance, his clothing, and the way he had transitioned into the spiritual realm. My friend was taken aback, and this experience confirmed for me that the presence I felt was real and protective, not just a figment of my imagination.

My friend's face went ashen grey and he quickly snatched back his wallet. "I believe you," he said. "I've heard enough."

My friend now appeared visibly shaken by this experience and I stopped the connection. Later my friend told me that the wallet had been given to him and had belonged to the man I had just described, my description had been accurate of the man he had once worked with. He continued to tell me that the man had died suddenly of a heart attack whilst at work, which explained the slight tightness I had felt in my chest when sharing his energy.

That evening after my friend left, I felt so good inside, this energy was amazing I could not sleep all night, I felt so alive.

This one experience deeply motivated and energised me, igniting a desire to explore more about the spiritual world. I suddenly felt this unstoppable urge to connect with others and help them find their way to healing and guidance. So, naturally, I threw myself into researching local spiritual churches and gatherings, determined to follow this new calling. Before long, I became a regular at these meetings, where I started offering messages to people who were searching for comfort and a little clarity in their lives.

At these gatherings, I met all kinds of people – some grieving, others just trying to figure out life. Many were hoping to reconnect with loved ones they'd lost, wanting to feel their presence or reignite that energy that had slipped away. There were also those who came in feeling completely stuck, looking for any kind of sign to reassure them that their loved ones were keeping an eye on things from above. Honestly, I could feel the energy in the room shifting with every story, and I found myself drawn to it, like I was part of something bigger (cue the dramatic music).

After a few months of participating in these spiritual meetings, I met a seasoned spiritual advisor. She gave me an important piece of advice: I needed to be cautious about the negative energy that I might attract. She explained that as I engaged with the spiritual realm, I could unknowingly invite in dark or negative energy. This kind of energy could drain the positive, light energy that I was trying to cultivate and share.

At the time, I had no clue what she was talking about. Negative energy? Darkness? Recharging my light? I mean, I was just riding the high of all this healing love, feeling like I was plugged into some cosmic energy source. But her words stuck with me, and while I didn't quite understand how to handle the darker side of things,

I knew this journey was going to be more than just sunshine and rainbows. But hey, I've always been up for a challenge!

Then, without any warning – boom – my focus snapped back to "real life". The daily grind came rushing in, and suddenly, all that light and excitement I'd been basking in was gone. It was like someone had flipped a switch. The joy of just being alive had faded into a shadow of itself, and honestly, I had no idea why.

Something inside me had shifted. I found myself letting go of that "too good to be true" energy that had once driven me. The spiritual curiosity that had kept me going now took a back seat, as I convinced myself that I just didn't have time for it anymore. Besides, constantly asking my dad to step in for extra babysitting duties was starting to feel like a bit much – even for him.

I made the conscious choice to ignore my inner guidance, convincing myself that focusing on home life and my nursing career was the "responsible" thing to do. It was like I'd turned down the volume on my intuition until it became nothing more than background noise, and eventually, it just disappeared entirely. I couldn't feel that spiritual connection anymore. It was as if the light had been switched off in every corner of my life.

Caught up in the grind, I jumped back on the career treadmill, chasing the next rung on the ladder like so many before me. I worked harder than ever, striving to make changes in the world around me, and pouring my energy into advancing professionally. But in the process, I was completely ignoring the quiet, powerful voice within – the one that had been guiding me so clearly before. Instead, my ego-driven, fear-based mind took over. It slid right back into the driver's seat, ready to steer me with logic and practicality. My inner dialogue became all about responsibilities. "You have a son to care for. This is your top priority. You don't have time for anything else."

I had unknowingly stepped away from that natural flow of life I had once trusted so deeply and retreated to something more familiar. It was a comfortable, but limiting, pattern – one rooted in scarcity and fear, where I'd find myself constantly focusing on what I lacked, rather than the abundance and possibilities that had once felt so real. I had swapped the excitement of self-discovery for the safety net of routine, telling myself it was the only way forward.

My focus returned to what I had always relied on to get me through: my job and my nurse training path. Extra training meant three-month placements on each new ward. I gave it all my energy and attention and a further year passed me by.

The Prowler

During my extra training that year, I was assigned to a psychiatric day unit – a place where patients from the local community would drop in for their medication, a cup of tea, a game of pool, or simply to socialise and participate in counselling and coaching sessions. It was a routine I had grown accustomed to – comforting even, in its predictability. But one afternoon, after finishing my early shift, something shattered that sense of routine.

As I approached my front door, I felt a strange sensation – an instinct, perhaps – that I wasn't alone. Turning around, my heart skipped a beat. Standing at the bottom of the path, just outside my front gate, was one of the patients from the unit. He wasn't supposed to be there. He shouldn't have known where I lived. He simply stood there, staring, a smirk tugging at the corners of his mouth as he locked eyes with me. Then, as casually as if it were the most normal thing in the world, he turned and walked away, disappearing down the road.

I tried to brush it off, telling myself it was just a coincidence. Maybe he lived nearby. Maybe it was nothing. But deep down, I couldn't shake the feeling that it was more than that.

A few days later, that unease returned with full force. I was at the local shops, standing in line, minding my own business, when I suddenly felt an unnervingly close presence behind me. My skin prickled. Slowly, I turned around, and there he was – those same piercing eyes. He was standing so close I could feel his breath on my neck. His stare wasn't just unsettling; it was invasive, cutting into me like a blade. My heart raced, and I didn't dare speak. I just pushed past him, my body on autopilot, desperate to get away.

What I had chalked up to a coincidence now felt like something far more sinister. He started showing up everywhere I went, his silent, unnerving gaze following me like a shadow. At work, I made a point to steer clear of him, shifting to the far side of the room whenever he was near. But the tension gnawed at me, growing stronger with every passing day. I knew I should tell someone, but the fear of losing my placement – or worse, being seen as overreacting – kept me quiet. I couldn't risk jeopardising the progress I'd worked so hard to make in my training.

Then, the next day, desperate for some relief, I confided in my next-door neighbour. I'll never forget the look on his face when he said he'd noticed someone peering through my bedroom window late one night. At first, I laughed it off he had a dry sense of humour that always threw me off – but the thought of someone lurking outside my home, watching me in the dark, sent a cold shiver down my spine. I was officially freaked out.

That night, paranoia took root and wouldn't let go. I triple-checked every window and every door, making sure each one was securely locked. My two-year-old son, Ben, slept soundly in his room, blissfully unaware of the dread that had its claws in me, replaying worst-case scenarios over and over in my mind. Days turned into weeks, and as my placement at the unit neared its end, I clung to the hope that once I moved on, this nightmare would be over. I would report him, and that would be that.

But the nightmare wasn't over. Not even close.

One evening, after tucking Ben into bed, I sat alone in the living room, the flicker of the TV casting eerie shadows across the walls. Outside, the autumn wind howled, its cold breath rattling the patio doors. Then I heard it – a noise, faint at first but unmistakable, coming from the patio doors behind me. My heart stopped and every muscle in my body tensed as I strained to hear. There it was again, louder this time, a deliberate sound, like someone testing the lock.

Panic surged through me. Without thinking, I bolted to the kitchen, grabbing the largest knife I could find. It felt surreal, like I had been preparing for this moment all along, dreading it but knowing, deep down, it was inevitable. But this wasn't some nightmare I could wake up from. This was real. And I was alone.

Knife in hand, I rushed back to the living room, holding my breath as I approached the blinds. My heart pounded so loudly that I was sure it would give me away. With trembling hands, I yanked the blinds open.

And there he was.

A dark figure stood just beyond the glass; his face hidden behind a mask. Only his eyes were visible – those same, cold, piercing eyes that had haunted me for weeks. His gaze met mine, unblinking, deliberate, sending a wave of icy fear through my body. For a moment, everything stopped. The knife shook in my grip, my legs felt like lead, and I couldn't move. I wanted to scream, but nothing came out, my throat tightened as terror swallowed me whole.

Adrenaline surged, but it didn't empower me – it paralysed me. My thoughts raced: if he got in, he could easily overpower me, take the knife, and I'd be helpless. My son was just a room away. No one would ever know until it was too late.

I forced my legs to move and stumbled toward the phone. My hands shook so violently I could barely pick up the receiver, and when I did, my mind went blank. It took a second for the emergency number to come to me. I punched in 999, heart hammering, as I turned back toward the patio doors.

The figure was gone. He had moved, slowly, almost casually, disappearing over the garden wall like he had all the time in the world. I didn't know whether to feel relief or panic.

Just as I started to catch my breath, the doorbell rang. I jumped, but then came the sound of familiar voices – police. My next-door neighbour had seen the intruder and called them before I even had the chance to dial.

The officers swept through the flat while Ben, miraculously, slept through the entire ordeal. When they knocked on his door, he stirred slightly, but I scooped him up and hugged him tight, trying to calm my racing heart. Relief and fear swirled together, the gravity of what had nearly happened sinking in. We had come so close to something unthinkable.

The next day, I reported the incident to my nurse tutor. Her concern was immediate, insisting I take time off to recover – both physically and mentally. I realised then how reckless I'd been, putting my career and training above everything else, even my own safety, even Ben's. I should have spoken up sooner. I should have acted before it escalated to this.

That day, I made a promise to myself: I would never let anything jeopardise our safety again.

My nurse tutor took swift action, contacting both the local police and the council housing department, urging them to work together to ensure my protection. The police increased patrols in the area, and the housing department began looking into options to enhance the security of my flat. It was a relief to know that steps were being taken to safeguard us, but the fear still lingered, a constant reminder of how fragile our sense of security can be.

As I sat in the quiet of my home, I realised how close I had come to being a victim of my own silence. The experience left me shaken, but also stronger, and more determined than ever to trust my instincts and protect what truly mattered – my son, my safety, and our future.

The police reassured me they would be patrolling my area each night and keeping a close watch on my flat. Despite this, the prowler – always masked, always silent – continued his night-time visits. He seemed to relish the fear he caused, standing just outside the patio doors, his piercing eyes locked on mine through the glass. It felt like a twisted game he was playing, one where the rules were meant to keep me on edge, trapped in my own home.

Though I had no solid proof, every instinct told me this was the same man from the psychiatric day unit.

But what could I say?

That he stared at me?

That his eyes were terrifyingly intense?

He hadn't spoken a word, hadn't made any overt threats, just followed me, appearing wherever I was.

It felt impossible to explain to anyone without sounding paranoid or overreacting. Yet, I knew deep down that this man intended to frighten me, and he was succeeding.

The fear wrapped around me, tightening its grip with every visit. I felt exposed, vulnerable, and controlled – like a puppet being manipulated by invisible strings. The situation dredged up old wounds, triggering memories of my childhood when I had felt similarly trapped, desperate to hide and become invisible. Those familiar feelings of helplessness washed over me, and all I wanted was to escape, to disappear from his sight.

Four long weeks passed, each one more draining than the last. Then the local council contacted me with news that felt like a blow to the chest. They had decided, along with my manager and the police, that I would be moved out of my flat and re-housed in a different area. The decision was made to protect my safety, but it felt like a punishment. I was being forced to leave the only home my son had ever known, the place I had carefully built for us.

The following week, I packed up our lives and said a reluctant goodbye to the flat that had once been a sanctuary. As we drove away, the weight of the change settled heavily on my shoulders. My life had been uprooted overnight. I was now distanced from the family support, my dad I had always relied on, and cut off from my work, which had been conveniently close to where we lived. My ideal setup was gone, replaced by an unfamiliar environment where I felt isolated and alone.

Settling into our new place was difficult. The walls of the unfamiliar house felt cold and unwelcoming. I spent sleepless nights listening for any sound, any sign that the nightmare had followed us. But as the days passed, I slowly began to realise that the prowler had stayed behind. The visits stopped, but the fear lingered, a shadow that refused to fade.

Though I was physically safe, the emotional scars remained. I couldn't shake the feeling of being watched, even in this new place. Every time I walked past a window or heard an unexpected noise, my heart would race, expecting to see those eyes staring back at me. I was out of my comfort zone, isolated with my two-and-a-half-year-old son and struggling to adjust to this new reality.

But in the quiet moments, when I allowed myself to breathe, I felt a different kind of strength beginning to surface. I had survived this ordeal, and although it had left me shaken, it hadn't broken me. I had protected my son, even when it meant giving up everything that was familiar. In that small but significant victory, I found a glimmer of hope. I began to understand that this move, though forced, was also a chance to rebuild and start over in a place where the shadows of the past couldn't follow.

As I unpacked the last of our belongings, I made a promise to myself. This time, I wouldn't let fear control my life. I would reclaim the sense of security and peace I had lost and although it would take time, I knew that I would find my footing again, stronger and wiser from the experience.

Takeaway Lesson

This experience taught me the crucial importance of trusting my instincts and prioritising my safety and wellbeing, even when it feels inconvenient or disruptive. It's easy to second-guess ourselves, especially when the threats we face aren't obvious or easily explained. But ignoring those gut feelings can lead to dangerous situations. I learned that it's okay to ask for help, to take action when something doesn't feel right, and to make difficult decisions to protect what truly matters (my safety and that of my son). Sometimes, the most empowering choice we can make is to walk away from what's familiar to find a safer, more secure environment. In doing so, we reclaim our power and take the first steps toward healing and rebuilding our lives on our own terms.

Chapter Five
Moving On to Pastures New

I moved just five miles away to a two-bedroom council house, but the struggle persisted. I was constantly tired, juggling mixed day and night shifts.

Money was always tight, and I could never seem to make enough. I accepted second-hand furniture with gratitude, though it came with guilt and shame. The mismatched pieces clashed in my new home, but they served their purpose. My furniture looked like I felt: old, worn out, and barely holding together.

I managed to get hold of an old car for work and every day I held my breath as I turned the key, especially in winter. Miraculously, it always started – just like I did, somehow scraping by.

Even its yearly MOTs passed without needing major repairs, a small victory in a life full of struggles.

Life had become a relentless treadmill, a constant grind of working full-time just to keep the lights on and food on the table. My days were a blur of responsibilities, from taking care of my young son, who I could finally afford to send to nursery, to feeding Benson, my large German Shepherd dog, who I had recently rescued and couldn't bear to give up. The weight of it all pressed down on me so hard that I often skipped meals, replacing dinner with roll-up cigarettes. They were my guilty pleasure, my only coping mechanism.

I was a nurse and a single mother, roles that should have made me proud, but deep down, I never felt like I was enough. The job, at least, provided me with a sense of purpose and some form of a social life. At work, I could put on a mask and pretend everything was fine. I was trusted, I worked hard, and I genuinely enjoyed helping people – listening to their stories and understanding how life had led them to physical illness.

The hospital was a place where I could momentarily escape my own chaos.

But when the workday ended, and the façade faded, I was left with a life that felt like it was unravelling. On the rare weekends or evenings when I could indulge, I'd buy a couple of bottles of the cheapest wine I could find. The first sip was always bitter, but after a few glasses, the bitterness faded, replaced by a numbness that dulled the exhaustion and anger simmering inside me. That brief escape was all I had, a fleeting moment of relief from a reality I had grown to despise.

I hated everything: the rundown house, the second-hand furniture, the toxic relationships that seemed to cling to me like shadows. My life was a chaotic mess, a tangle of disappointments and bad decisions. It felt like everything happened to me, not for me. Life was something I endured, not something I lived. And as I trudged through each day, I couldn't shake the feeling that I was attracting this chaos, like a magnet pulling in negativity with every thought and every word I spoke. I was stuck in a loop, a vicious cycle that kept spinning me back into the same chaos. And I couldn't stop complaining, even though deep down, I knew it wouldn't change anything.

But then, one morning, something strange happened. I woke up feeling… happy. It was a rare, almost alien sensation, but it was real. That glimmer of happiness made me pause and realise how desperately I needed to change my life. I couldn't keep living the same day over and over, trapped in a cycle of struggle and despair. Something had to give.

That morning, I made a decision. I had to start asking myself what I really wanted out of life. I needed to stop repeating the same mistakes, to break free from the patterns that had kept me locked in place. It was the beginning of a shift, though I didn't fully understand it at the time.

Not long after that, on one of those rare nights out with friends, I met someone new. He was charming, and for the first time in a long while, I felt seen/visible. Looking back, I realise how vulnerable I was, how much I craved connection, any connection. He became my boyfriend quickly, too quickly, perhaps, but I was lonely, desperate for something to change. After a few months, he moved in with me and my little family.

It felt like a new beginning but deep down I knew I was repeating old patterns, clinging to someone else to fill the void inside me. I wanted to believe that things were finally getting better, but a part of me knew that I was still running on that same treadmill, just with a different backdrop.

My desperation to be with someone to bring me happiness brought with it a familiar package: *patterns* of control and jealousy delivered in emotional abuse. This pattern or lesson was being repeated but this time I was more aware of it. I could see the pattern, but I still needed to learn the lesson that would help me to break it, however, it felt easier to carry on ignoring the cracks and I continued to push down how I truly felt.

At least I was with someone! I told myself this, allowing it to subconsciously manifest what felt familiar even though it was not what I truly wanted or deserved. It was my comfort zone.

It's like having that double helping of cake when you know you want to lose weight, then you continue with the same comfort foods default patterns, giving up on what you really want – your goal, to feel good and be fit and healthy.

My inner critic had become my constant companion, always ready to pounce, but this time it served a purpose, pulling me back from the brink of despair and urging me to focus on what I knew best: my job.

Work became my refuge, a sanctuary where I could escape the suffocating reality of my crumbling relationship. At home, I poured all my energy into caring for Ben and walking Benson in the park, finding comfort in those simple routines.

Then, out of the blue, came an opportunity that seemed like a lifeline, a fast-track course that could propel me to the top of my nursing career. Securing a place on that course felt like a dream finally within reach. This was it, the moment I had worked so hard for. I was on the brink of becoming a highly qualified nurse, and I told myself that once I achieved this, everything else in my life would naturally fall into place.

For six gruelling months, I juggled motherhood, work, and relentless study sessions. Every night, after putting Ben to bed, I would sit down with my books, drowning in guilt as my boyfriend's demands and complaints grew louder. He resented the time I dedicated to my studies, insisting that I wasn't giving him the attention he deserved. The tension in the house was unbearable, but I pressed on, determined to succeed.

The night before my final exam, the pressure reached a boiling point. What should have been a night of quiet preparation exploded into a massive argument. It was the final straw for him. He packed his things and left, slamming the door on our relationship and my last shred of emotional support. I was devastated. How could he do this to me the night before the most important exam of my life?

I didn't sleep that night. I watched the clock tick away the hours, feeling utterly broken and unsure if I could face the exam the next day. But as morning broke, something deep inside me stirred, a flicker of resilience I didn't know I had. I decided I had to go, I had to sit that exam no matter how shattered I felt.

When I arrived at the exam centre, I was a shell of myself, numb and disconnected. I took my seat, and as the tutor pressed the clock to begin, the room's silence became suffocating. I stared at the paper, paralysed by fear. Then, as if to amplify my dread, the girl next to me turned over her paper, glanced at the questions, and bolted from the room. I wanted to do the same. My inner critic screamed at me to give up, to run away, but I stayed.

My heart pounded, my hands shook, and uncontrolled waves of emotions threatened to drown me. Slowly, I turned the exam paper over, reminding myself that this was the most important test of my life. My first few lines were barely legible, my handwriting a frantic scrawl as if my thoughts were trying to escape. But as the minutes ticked by, I found my rhythm. The panic subsided, my hand steadied, and I fell into a flow state. Words began to pour out of me, clear and confident.

Before I knew it, it was over. I had completed the four-hour exam. I sat back, took a deep breath, and felt a wave of relief wash over me. For the first time in months, I could relax, knowing I had done everything I could. Now, all I could do was wait six long weeks until the results would arrive.

But at that moment, I had already won a personal battle. I hadn't run away. I had faced the storm head-on, and that felt like a victory in itself.

The time quickly passed. During this time, the toxic boyfriend returned with a bunch of flowers, a bottle of wine, and chocolates, asking for forgiveness and for me to take him back. I did. I blamed myself, I felt like I was the guilty party, the one at fault. Shortly after we got back together, he moved back in, and I fell back into the familiar *pattern* – still trying to work out the lesson – and focusing on trying to make the toxic relationship I found myself in work.

Results day in every way!

Unable to sleep all night, by the morning of results day, I had my fifth cup of coffee in hand. I was standing in the living room when I heard the post fall onto the inside floor in the hallway. My boyfriend quickly went and picked up the post and shuffled through the brown bill envelopes until he found the results envelope addressed to me. He came into the room and thrust it into my hands for me to open.

"Not yet," I said, "I'm scared."

"Just open it," he said.

Feeling nervous and pressured, and with shaking hands, I opened the letter and read the first sentence: *Congratulations…*

I shouted out, "I've passed!"

He looked at me in disbelief, his mouth tightening at each corner. "You've passed? After what I put you through?" He quickly realised what he had just verbalised out loud.

It was too late. The penny had finally dropped.

And there it was shown to me, I had learnt the lesson and passed more than one exam that day.

This confirmed I had not imagined it, my critical voice telling me I was in the wrong, and all along it had been him that was controlling me. He didn't want the best for me, he wanted me to fail, to keep me trapped. I was done with that – he had to go. That day I realised how little he cared for my happiness and how little I cared about it for myself.

Takeaway Lesson

Lonely and in need of love, I craved attention and feared rejection, repeating and attracting the same relationships that lacked the happiness I was looking for.

Effectively the same partner but in a different package meant I kept attracting what I didn't want on repeat. I had been stuck in my fantasy of love and only experienced unhappiness. This wasn't love I was receiving or giving to myself.

I now had a different choice to make.

Chapter Six
Completion and Changes

After years of dedication and hard work, I had finally reached my destination in my nursing career, a place I had dreamed of for so long. Standing on that stage, diploma in hand, I was officially a top-rank nurse, my name proudly etched into the nursing register. The ceremony was everything I had imagined, a celebration of my perseverance and achievement.

But as I stood there, dressed in my mother's ill-fitting dress because I couldn't afford one of my own, a mix of emotions swirled within me. The excitement of my success was tempered by an unexpected discomfort. Even my mother's reluctant presence without a word of praise couldn't dampen my spirits for long. I had done it; I had achieved my BIG goal. So why did I feel like something was still missing? As the initial euphoria faded, I realised that I was at a crossroads. I had achieved my career goal and felt empty.

Looking at my life I realised I'd spent so many years focused on rescuing others – not just in my job role but family, friends, even broken relationships – that I had lost sight of myself. I had poured my energy into healing others' pain, only to realise that my family and some friends weren't ready to be healed. They clung to their suffering, unwilling to let go, and in their pain, I remained trapped – stuck in the same cycle of comfort and chaos, unable to break free.

But something had shifted within me. I began to see things clearly for the first time. This was no longer the life I wanted. I had changed. I no longer felt the need to please everyone around me. I started to distance myself from those who drained my energy, and as I did, I noticed something remarkable. People's attitudes towards me began to change. Those who once felt comfortable around me now seemed threatened, their body language was stiff, and their eyes avoided mine. This was new territory for me. For the first time, I wasn't suffocating under the weight of others' expectations. Instead, I felt a newfound confidence, a courage to break free from the past and the limiting beliefs that had held me captive for so long.

It was time to focus on me, to undo the patterns that had kept me trapped, and to step into the life I was truly meant to live. The question wasn't "What next?" but rather, "Who do I want to become now that I have freed myself?"

A lightbulb moment that lit up my awareness had occurred, the only way I could help anyone else heal was to start by healing myself. Only once I had made my own changes and followed my own path. But it had to start with me, and I felt this was the right time to change.

It took some time, and I felt alone as I distanced myself from those friends, but I started asking myself better questions about what I truly wanted in my life, and I intuitively opened up to receive new ideas and solutions.

A powerful, lighter energy reignited within me a deep connection to my intuitive guidance and a renewed sense of positivity. For the first time in a long while, I felt truly alive, fully present in the 'moment'. Embracing this newfound clarity, I committed to creating a new reality rooted in my own wellbeing. I became deeply interested in cultivating calm, exploring relaxation techniques, and practising meditation to support my journey.

As I unravelled the layers of my mind, I began to seriously redefine who I wanted to be, discovering the authentic self I had longed to uncover.

Takeaway Lesson

Don't ever be afraid of losing people, be afraid of losing yourself by trying to fit in and please everybody else. Be true to yourself. When you stay true and tune in to your intuitive 'true self' all the right people will show up on the higher positive energy frequency, just trust and have faith that You are never alone.

Having had time to reflect, it became apparent that when it came to my career, I had a clear vision and made my own decisions. I knew without doubt I could and would achieve my desire to be a nurse and complete my dream, my goal. I had no resistance, and I had faith over fear throughout my nurse training. I aligned and focused on what I believed would be my outcome. I visualised my future self in the uniform I would be wearing and how it would feel.

That became my reality.

Chapter Seven
Friendships Revisited, Renewed, and Completed

I'd achieved my nurse goal and continued to give myself space away from friends and family. But I also continued to feel something was missing in my life. There was something inside telling me that I had more to do, but what was it?

Having space for the first time in my life, and leaving behind my close circle, I had mixed feelings. Sometimes I felt lost and confused, and other times I continued to focus on feeling happy and finding my missing piece to uncover more of ME. This was a constant emotional rollercoaster, with every new question leading to more ups and downs.

Who was I other than my identity of being a nurse and mother? I was determined to find out what else I could be and do, so I set out on a journey to find it.

Where or how would I start this journey of finding me? One afternoon I spent some time alone and thought back to my childhood and when I was truly happy, free and having fun in my life. While I was thinking about my childhood friends and my first best friend, Lynn, and our happy times, suddenly the phone rang. On answering, I couldn't believe it: it was her voice on the phone, she had called me out of the blue.

"I was just thinking about you," I said.

"We must be on the same energy frequency," she replied.

However, everything changed with that call. It was not long after Lynn had joyfully welcomed her fourth child into the world, and now her voice, trembling and broken, delivered the devastating news: she had been diagnosed with terminal breast cancer.

As her words sank in, a flood of memories from our childhood rushed back to me – Lynn's deepest, darkest fear had come true. I could vividly recall the nights she would cry to me, terrified that she would one day face the same fate as her mother. Now, that nightmare had become her reality. My mind went blank, overwhelmed by the weight of her pain. She sobbed on the other end of the line, but this time I was paralysed – unable to console her, unable to find the right words, helpless in the face of a fear that had finally taken form.

I remember thinking I had to be strong and show her no sadness or fear in response to her news. It took so much effort to concentrate and keep a steady tone in my voice as I responded to her news and distress. At the end of the call, the emotional energy I had held in my body made me feel exhausted and I collapsed onto the bed in despair.

The following morning, I decided I needed to rest and process this news. I made up my mind that I would be her strength to fight this and be by her side every step of the way in every way I could. The following weeks turned into months, and I stayed close in the background, feeling helpless but not wanting to be in the way of her family time after she had completed the long cycles of chemotherapy.

Within six months, Lynn had been admitted to hospital for palliative care. I needed to be there for her, I just didn't know how or when the right time would be to visit her. Would I be in the way?

She was constantly on my mind and every day I would meditate and send healing her way.

It was in July, after meditation one morning and whilst getting ready for my day ahead, that a powerful feeling washed over me, followed by an unmistakable inner voice: *Visit Lynn.*

I looked around the room. I had a strange feeling like someone was in the room with me, goosebumps covered my body and I shivered with what felt like ice prickling my skin. Lynn had been in hospital for two weeks and I had not visited her yet but for the rest of that morning, all I could think about was her. As the morning went on, the feeling got stronger, and by lunchtime, I'd made the decision to go and visit.

I remember arriving on that sunny summer's day and finding a car park space so easily – the parking angels were on my side as it was rare to find an empty space at that time of day in a cancer care hospital. Normally I would drive around for at least half an hour, due to the car park always being full with people travelling across the country for treatments, and visitors needing spaces.

I parked up, purchased a ticket and set off. On reaching the main hospital entrance I was greeted by Lynn's husband outside the doors having a coffee break, he let out a sigh of relief and said, "She's had a rough morning. I'm glad you've come. Go up and sit with her."

I nodded in agreement and took the lift to the second floor, walked onto the ward, double-checked her name and bed number on the familiar nursing station name board, and made my way to the side room where she was.

On opening the door, I saw her two young sons sitting at one side of her bed, and on the other side, an empty chair where her husband had been sitting. I went to the empty chair and sat beside her. Her mouth was frothing, and her eyes were rolling and disappearing into her eyelids. I took hold of her hand, called her name, and her eyes rolled down to fix on mine.

It was as if she had been waiting for me, and deep down I knew she had been.

"I'm here now, Lynn," I said.

As I held her hand in mine, I wiped her mouth and told her she would be okay. She stared into my eyes then a few seconds later closed her eyes and peacefully slipped away.

That day, that minute, my heart broke into a million bits for the second time. Losing her this time there would be no repair. They say time is a great healer, but the scars remain, and the memories never fade of my first true friendship. It was the best I ever made.

The Anger Years

After losing Lynn, I disconnected from my intuition and inner voice. Anger consumed me, and I forgot what it meant to truly feel – I went numb.

I remember being suddenly gripped by strong emotions of grief. I wanted to run away but there was nowhere to hide. Life continued as usual for everyone else but inside I was furious. How could the world move on when my own felt shattered? It took me years to realise that

I was projecting my deepest feelings of anger onto those around me as I tried to stay in control. Sometimes this resulted in a mishmash of chaotic feelings and emotions, some of them my own and some picked up from those around me. I slipped back into default mode, working hard as a nurse and letting my inner critic become my constant companion.

My son and my job were the two pinpricks of light in a life that was otherwise dark. My bittersweet life experiences continued, two years passed, I was just drifting along when suddenly Kevin (my first boyfriend) came back into my life in an unexpected way.

Kevin was admitted to the ward where I worked after being brutally assaulted and robbed on a night out. He suffered a severe concussion and head injury, leaving him disoriented and broken. It was such a shock to see him so badly beaten and confused. The head injury left Kevin with long-term epilepsy, a life sentence of medication and uncertainty. This gentle man I had known was forever changed.

Not long after recovering and leaving hospital, Kevin started to change. His DJ identity had been taken away, he became depressed and, living alone, he found life difficult to deal with. He started going out drinking large amounts of alcohol most weekends. Our relationship changed and roles reversed. I was now the one trying to rescue him.

I would constantly check in and call the flat on my days off work or at weekends. It took time, I wanted to be there for him and help with healing his pain, and it seemed to be working. He started to accept the new daily medication that he had been prescribed, accepting and understanding it would prevent any further fits or complications. Eventually, he got back to normal work/life balance, returning to his day job, mixing with friends and getting support from family. I felt relieved that at last he had turned a corner, and life had started to look good for him once more.

Six weeks later, everything shattered. Kevin came home alone after a night of drinking and never saw the morning. He suffered an epileptic fit that claimed his life.

When they told me the next day, they said it likely happened without warning – or maybe because he was drunk, he didn't notice the signs. But I couldn't accept that.

There were scratches on the inside of the front door, deep and desperate, made by his fingernails. They spoke of his final moments, the raw, terrifying fight to open that door, to raise the alarm, to survive.

I replayed that scene endlessly in my mind, a nightmare on a loop. Kevin, scared and alone, dying in silence.

Why was he taken so suddenly?

Why didn't I get to say goodbye?

The grief crushed me, a familiar ache that returned with a vengeance, but still, no tears came – only a deep, seething anger. It was as if my heart had grown used to breaking; the pain of an unwanted companion that wouldn't let go. I wanted to hide, to pull away from the world that had become so cruel. Everyone I loved, everyone I let in, seemed to be ripped away from me. It felt like a curse. Kevin had promised he'd always be there for me, and I had believed him. But then, just like that, he was gone.

When the funeral day arrived I could not stop my tears. The tears that had been absent all these years, now rolled down my face, out of control, as I planted my chosen flowers on the fresh topsoil of his grave. These flowers, so significant in our relationship, were memories of when we first met. They were from my favourite song – the one Kevin always played for me when we first met: "Send me forget-me-nots." These were the delicate blue flowers I now planted and watered with my salty tears.

Many years after this, these familiar delicate flowers grew in my garden. I must admit I was a little confused but pleasantly surprised to see these flowers for the first time. It made me smile, showing early spring. They were in my garden without me ever intentionally planting them, and yet these beautiful flowers appeared for me to see, between the weeds, every spring every year going forward. I knew it was Kevin's way of letting me know he would always be with me, be near me, and as a way of saying he was okay.

Takeaway Lesson

Life reflected back at me like a mirror, showing a mind overgrown with weeds – negative fear patterns and beliefs rooted in grief. I had started to distrust the possibility of anything good happening in my life.

Yet there was hope. I didn't see it at first, but the flowers appeared, revealing the contrast between life and loss. It would take years before I fully understood, but those flowers were a sign that change was possible, and I would one day change my thinking and create a new life.

It's one thing to believe we have a powerful mind, but it's another to know how to shift it into the right gear – to use it to transform our lives.

But in time, I would learn how – because I was willing to fight for it.

Chapter Eight
The Transition Years:
Giving Up – Getting Up

Even though it was spring outside, my dark days continued. I carried on drowning in a heavy sea of negative energy that consumed me, aged me, even stole my passion for life. I stopped caring how I looked physically or how or what I *felt* inside. It felt like I was addicted to the stress, as if cortisol itself had taken over, sending my mind and body into a chaotic, uncontrollable spiral.

My life became an ongoing daily hangover.

In my personal life, I had defaulted and recycled old patterns on repeat, continuing to attract loveless toxic relationships, trying to make them work, allowing myself to be a puppet, emotionally dead and psychologically controlled, back to agreeing with everyone else's opinions and accepting the blame if anything went wrong. It was as if I needed to be punished to feel better. I continued to spend my time running away from my thoughts and feelings by self-medicating on the cheap bottles of wine and smoking endless cigarettes. They were a way to escape, to feel better, and to be accepted and valued by those around me. Endless cups of coffee kept me going throughout each tough day. Life was hard.

At the time, I couldn't see a way forward out of the pattern I found myself in; I wasn't aware it could be any different. It felt like I was on life support, just about breathing. I was angry and in self-destruct mode. I just didn't care.

My inner critical voice played freely in my mind, reminding me I was invisible in the crowd, I didn't matter. Each day I slipped deeper into victim mode, allowing myself to travel into the depths of my problems and creating further undesired situations. However, deep inside there was that familiar old friend, a small intuitive inner voice trying to communicate with me. It wanted to shout out loud and be seen. It wanted to be set free, but at the time, I didn't know how to set it free and move forward to be me. I pushed it back down.

> *"We cannot solve our problems with the same thinking and energy we used when we created them."*
> *– Albert Einstein*

I had evolved into a great actress in life, just like when I was a child faking illness to avoid school. This time I was playing the roles I thought people wanted me to be. I was pretending. Anyone looking at my life from the outside would see everything looked fine. I was always smiling and cracking jokes, I was the clown who cheered people up and never let them down. The people pleaser once more, being there for friends and family so they could feel better and secure. In work and at home, I was a great all-rounder giving my time and energy, taking their bad days away. Once I was alone, feeling empty inside, I felt isolated and closed the door to my inner home.

Being a nurse was the easy part. I loved it with a passion, I felt alive, and I had been trained to have clear boundaries, not get emotionally close or involved, to keep in check any emotional response and not show true feelings. That was part of the job role, especially when caring for patients, young children, and older people who had terminal illnesses or who died.

Over time, I had become emotionally desensitised. Working in the NHS was both busy and rewarding, situations were ever-changing. I was often in charge of busy wards; to make extra money I would regularly work extra agency shifts covering most wards in the local general hospital.

Doing this stopped me thinking about my life and drinking it away. Working as a nurse was, after all, my purpose at that time, my drive to keep going, plus I gained lots of valuable experience and could choose where I wanted to work.

Eventually, I chose to work on a surgical ward full-time.

Each morning I'd get up and be ready to leave at 6 a.m. to drop Ben off before school at his grandparents' house so I could start my nurse shift on the ward at 7 a.m.

Ben was growing up, it had become easier to manage my work/life balance to work more, although I still never made enough money.

I always had credit card debts and used the cards for special occasions including what I called our 'special days' where once a year I would take Ben out from school, and we would go out together for the day. I allowed him to have whatever he wanted to eat and bought him whatever he asked for that was within reason (usually new football boots). Those days were such special times and memories that gave us time together to enjoy the day and talk. I guess it helped me feel less guilty about him not having a dad in his life, the choice I had made when I left Newcastle and broke all communication and ties. I always feared that, one day, Paul and his parents would come and take Ben away, they had money after all, and I didn't. But I had something more valuable to give – my deep love for him.

I realise now looking back why I feared money and never had enough at that time, I thought I had to choose between love or money!

Over the years the job I loved started to change, nursing was slowly changing, new nurses recruited were now trained at local universities, the focus being on academic study over practical experience on the wards, and student nurses became fewer in numbers on the nursing rota. Staff shortages and low recruitment started to be noticed, often I would be doing extra shifts working nights and weekends, and resentment started to set in for the first time in my nursing career.

The love affair with being a nurse and working in the NHS was over, I felt invisible every time I asked for extra support. I'd reached my limits in energy and passion. I started to feel like I could not make a difference alone. After years of studying and training to reach my lifelong goal, it had now lost all value and appeal.

Mountains of paperwork and new systems were introduced, and I felt they had become more important than the patients who needed nursing care and the focus of my time. Higher managers had lost interest and ignored my plea for help. I was dying inside. Everything I loved about being a nurse had been stripped away and my daily escape from the grind of my home life... now became something I dreaded.

One day, I snapped. Whilst sitting at the nurse's station, talking with the physio, I suddenly noticed the constant noise of nurse call bells and red lights: patients calling for assistance. I remember looking at the red lights and wanting to run away. I just didn't have enough energy or time to get up and respond to their calls, still having a mountain of paperwork in front of me to complete before handing over to the next shift. Without any warning, I felt tears starting to well in my eyes as I looked across at the patients' beds.

"I can't do this anymore, I'm leaving," I told the physio.

She looked at me in disbelief and said, "You can't leave, this is a secure job, how will you live?"

I didn't have any reply for her, but that day I quit anyway. As I walked out of the hospital, I felt such a release – like the pressure that had been building up inside me for years was finally lifting. It was like exhaling after holding my breath for too long. But even with that sense of freedom, I knew deep down this was the biggest gamble of my life. There was no safety net, no backup plan, and no certainty of what came next. All I knew was that I couldn't continue living in a way that left me drained and invisible. The fear of what I had just done pulsed beneath my relief, but for the first time in a long time,

I allowed myself to trust that something better could come.

With no savings or Plan B, I was forced to claim benefits, but I swore it was temporary and swallowed the feelings of guilt and shame whilst I searched for what to do next.

Priorities

My priorities had changed focus, I had always felt I had never had enough time to spend with Ben, hence the 'special day', but now more than ever I wanted this time with him. I needed to be at home. Being with him lifted my energy, put on a light that made my world real, and we had fun.

Football became his passion, and we would spend most weekends on the football pitch along with his best friend, Stee, who we nicknamed Sedge. I had unofficially adopted Stee. He was two years older than Ben, lived on the same road, and came from a household of five brothers. He needed to escape and have space for himself, and he found that space by spending time at our house.

Watching Ben and Stee's friendship reminded me of my own childhood with Lynn. Back then, life felt easy, filled with fun, laughter, and freedom. Those were the days when we could just be ourselves, without any worries or pretences. We played, we dreamed, and we were completely happy.

Takeaway Lesson

Looking back, I realise that those childhood friendships weren't just about having fun; they were lessons in resilience, trust, and authenticity. In a world that often demands we wear masks to fit in, those early bonds reminded me that it's the connections where we can truly be ourselves that sustain us through life's hardest moments. As I watched Ben and Stee's friendship flourish, I saw that same freedom I once had with my best friend, Lynn – where nothing mattered but the joy of being real and accepted for who we were.

Those friendships taught me that it's okay to step away from roles that don't serve us, to let go of expectations, and to prioritise what truly matters. They shaped how I guide Ben, encouraging him to nurture relationships that give him the space to be himself and to stay true to his passions – whether it's on the football pitch or in life. And perhaps most importantly, they reminded me that we're never truly alone as long as we hold on to the people who see us for who we really are.

Chapter Nine
The Universe Gave Me a Wakeup Call

After leaving nursing, I used the time and space to focus on what I really wanted in my life, and after a couple of months, I decided to explore courses to retrain. The benefits department encouraged and supported me to apply for a three-year course to retrain as a Person-Centred Counsellor.

Although I was scared and worried about not being good enough to do the training, it felt like it was a natural calling. I could help others like me because I understood pain and hardship, after all, I was an expert and living in it. Plus, this retraining programme would give me more time to be at home.

I had stepped out of my comfort zone and into the unknown. I remember being both excited and nervous about starting the counselling course. Unaware at the time that this would be my own healing journey along the way.

Two weeks after being accepted on the course, I found myself standing in the bookshop with my recommended reading list in hand, looking on the bookshelves for names of all the top masters in psychology. I felt so honoured to be there to learn the healing techniques for the mind from these masters.

Suddenly the Universe had other plans. A brightly coloured book on a far shelf seemed to almost glow, pulling me toward it. I went over, curiously picked the book out and randomly opened it. BAM! Something shifted inside me, subtle yet undeniable, as if I had just received a message I didn't even know I needed. I knew in that instant that this book was meant for me. Somewhere deep inside, I felt a shift I hadn't felt before. I instinctively knew that I had to buy this book. Excitement ran through every cell of my body thinking about having this book for my own. I didn't have enough money for all the books and struggled with which book to put back. Surely, I didn't need all the masters of psychology!

I decided I had to buy that book, and that one big decision changed my life.

Arriving home, excited with my purchases – and despite it being a very cold dull December day – I felt happy and content with my life, with a warm glow stirring inside me for the first time in as long as I can remember. That afternoon I sat and opened my newly purchased chosen book.

Wow. As I read the pages something huge happened – not externally, but internally, deep inside me – that was to change my mind and world forever. I suddenly saw my life through a completely different lens. Reading that book, I understood that the life I had at that time was one that I had created because of the way I was thinking about my life and myself. These thoughts gave me the emotions, feelings and behaviours that reinforced my thinking.

And... I now once again saw that I had the power within me to change everything. That afternoon, reading that book, time flew, and I nearly missed the school run to pick up Ben. I was engrossed in the book, like a sponge soaking up every sentence, every paragraph, and every page.

This book was talking to me, it held messages about me, and it touched something new deep inside. I completed the book that same day and it shifted my mood. I felt so good inside, energised for the first time in such a long time, so alive. What was this? I wasn't sure. Maybe it was because I was going out that evening, a rare occasion out with friends, celebrating Christmas and my new career path.

That evening was the 19th of December 2001. I will never forget it.

I had taken Ben to stay at his grandparents' house for a sleepover whilst I went out. The night was perfect, with lots of festive drinks, good food and company, along with the bright lights and decorations in the town and restaurant adding to the ambience. Everything was perfect.

Then the mood suddenly shifted. My feelings of happiness suddenly switched and tumbled down rapidly into despair. Barely two hours into the evening, it was cut short by a neighbour's alarming phone call.

"You need to get home. Your house is on fire."

I knew my son was safe with his grandparents but Benson the dog was still at home.

A rush of panic, anxiety and fear took over at great speed and I felt sick. I completely sobered up and was speechless for what felt like hours but was only seconds.

"Where's my dog?" I asked. "Can someone get my dog out?"

I learned that one brave neighbour had broken down the front door and had managed to coax Benson reluctantly downstairs and out to safety. Feeling some relief by the news that my dog was safe, I quickly took a taxi home. Turning into the road I was greeted by a crowd of people watching as the fire brigade had arrived and were getting ready to go into the house. I looked at the front windows – cracked and glass breaking under the pressure of the heat, bellowing out black smoke, with flames still lapping up the windows in the front room. I then noticed Benson sheepishly sitting in the garden, coughing and shaking – a pitiful sight for a large dog like him. I went over and hugged him, feeling such love and gratitude that he had survived.

Despite having no home insurance, I stood feeling surprisingly calm as I watched all my presents and Christmas tree being destroyed, as the final flames were dampened down. I continued to watch as the second-hand sofa, charred and only just recognisable, was dragged into the front garden. Then the house went into darkness. The front door to the house had been made secure and the fire service left along with the crowds, some of whom hugged me before going back safely behind their own front doors. I hugged my dog tightly, and I felt so lucky as we headed to my parents' house.

The following morning, I returned to witness the damage in the cold light of day. The front garden looked like I was stuck in a bad dream, old burnt-out shells of charcoal furniture and a black Christmas tree that had once been green. I had arrived to meet the fire officer who had come to meet and assess the safety of the property. He informed me I could move back into the property but only live in the upstairs part of the house, which was structurally safe.

With no house insurance and the bottom rooms destroyed by fire, I was grateful for the suggestion. Plus, I didn't have any other options.

As I walked with him into the living room which resembled a black cinder box, the only remaining piece of furniture was an old wooden coffee table standing in the centre of the room.

To my amazement, there on the floor was that one book, a little smoke-damaged but – unbelievably – it had survived the fire. I brushed off the black soot and the book's title showed me the sign yet again: *You Can Heal Your Life*.

Written by Louise Hay and originally published in 1984, the book presents the idea that our thoughts and beliefs have a direct impact on our physical and emotional health.

That day, as I wiped the soot from the front cover, I believed I could heal my life, I made a decision and started from that moment on.

Reading that book on the day of the fire had changed my life forever, including the way that I was able to process this disaster.

It made me realise that I had a choice about how to think and feel about this situation. I could be a victim and stay the same as I had always been, feeling sorry for myself, or I could think and believe I could have something different.

Using the power of positive thinking and reframing my mindset, I learned to release the stress and use affirmations to focus on what I truly wanted, rather than dwelling on what I didn't. Each day, I became more aware of the outdated patterns that once held me back. This newfound awareness filled me with confidence and a sense of empowerment, giving me the courage to pause and start a fresh chapter of my life. For the first time in my adult years, I felt truly free.

Using the power of positive thinking, reframing, letting go of the stress and using positive affirmations to affirm what I wanted in life, rather than affirming what I didn't want, I became consciously aware of those old, outdated patterns each day. This gave me a feeling of confidence and empowerment to pause and start a new chapter and adventure in my life.

In the aftermath of the fire, I realised I had lost so much more than just old, second-hand things that went up in flames that day. I had let go of a part of myself, the part that clung to anger, frustration, and negativity.

As I stood there, staring at the charred remains of what was once my home, it hit me: all the things I'd been bitterly complaining about, the resentment I held onto, had manifested in my life in ways I couldn't have predicted. It took losing everything to finally see that my own energy, my thoughts, and my words had played a role in shaping my reality.

Takeaway Lesson

The fire didn't just take my things, it took a version of me I didn't need any more. It forced me to see the habits and patterns that were holding me back. As I began to rebuild, I realised it wasn't just about replacing lost stuff; it was about reinventing myself. I had the chance to start over, not just with my home, but with my mindset. And that, more than anything, was the real gift I found in the ashes.

My life changed forever that December.

That Christmas we sat enjoying Christmas dinner, in the upstairs of a burnt house, sitting on striped deck chairs, and eating dinner on wooden boxes for tables. I felt appreciation and gratitude for my life and the simplicity that brought such happiness, I felt so lucky.

This fire had cleansed Me, and I had a blank canvas to create a different picture. In the new year, work would start on the cinder box living room downstairs.

Chapter Ten
Discovering ME

My mind reset, I started to build my new life. With new choices, the house felt completely different, and I could see life through a different lens once more, flowing with endless possibilities.

The new year arrived – January 2002 – and workmen were in and out, cleaning and plastering the blackened empty rooms downstairs. It took most of that month to complete and repair the smoke damage.

The smell of smoke lingered on clothes, hair and skin and seemed to remain forever in the house despite opening windows throughout the cold January days. Sitting on the striped deck chairs was now becoming uncomfortable and the novelty of eating sandwiches and watching a portable TV was getting more and more difficult to do with each passing day. It was no fun with a young boy and a large dog to look after. I certainly appreciated having a park nearby and we went daily to watch and play football and oxygenate ourselves with fresh air.

With the arrival of the new year, I had returned to my counselling course. I was surprised on the first day back to be told that in order to complete and pass the course and get the qualification, students had to attend a minimum of twenty personal therapy sessions and pay for them. I couldn't believe it! I felt so angry.

I remember thinking I don't have time or the money to be spending talking to a stranger for an hour each week. Plus, I'm training to be the helper, not the person who needs help. Plus, I don't have any problems so what would I talk about?

So, I refused.

But I was told in order to pass the course, I had to do it.

I reluctantly paid the money and had the sessions.

And I have to say... looking back, it was the best investment I have ever made.

At first, I couldn't see the value of sitting there talking about myself, and I thought who would be interested anyway? I'd always been told to just get on with my day and stop being emotional and needing attention, so I'd learned to completely ignore my feelings. But that was about to change.

About three or four weeks into the counselling, we were discussing money, and I told the counsellor that my new boyfriend at the time was trying to impress me. He'd completed a large building job and had given me two £50 notes and said, "Go and treat yourself."

I remember saying to the counsellor, "I've never actually held a real £50 note before. I've had that money in my purse for three weeks. I haven't a clue what to spend it on."

You see, apart from the cheap bottles of wine, I'd never spent money on me.

I didn't feel worth it. I didn't care about myself at all.

Working in those sessions and talking honestly about my feelings showed me that I had never valued or loved myself. I began to unravel the deep-rooted beliefs about money and self-worth that had kept me stuck in a cycle of scarcity and doubt which, in turn, had attracted more lack!

The counsellor challenged me to spend the two £50 notes on myself. This felt so uncomfortable and out of my normal way of being. I felt scared spending it on me because I didn't want to waste it. In the end, I spent it on some perfume. Each time I smelt that perfume it reminded me of the luxury treat I had given myself and I felt a warm glow inside.

That's also when I saw the counselling in a different way – because I knew that this was more than just passing a course. This was about caring for me, it was an investment in my happiness, which was key to having a different life. That one big decision to say 'yes' to those sessions rather than quit the course, continued opening and changing my path, allowing me to continue to create my new life.

I had paid such a small financial amount for the best life-changing gift that counselling gave me along this path to freedom and happiness.

It was a turning point that taught me the true meaning of value, both in terms of money and, more importantly, in terms of myself.

A Challenge for You:

As you read this, pause for a minute and notice what thoughts and feelings are coming up for you about money.

If you're feeling guilty when you spend money on yourself, then it shows that maybe there's some work for you to do too. What are you investing in?

Waking up to me

Those sessions had taken me out of my comfort zone and challenged everything about me and my life. I uncovered things I didn't even know about that were getting in the way of me living the life I wanted.

I had opened my mind and stretched my awareness, becoming in touch with a deeper part of me that had been ignored for such a long time. I learnt that I could have the best and happiest relationships, but first I had to discover how to have a relationship with myself.

Don't get me wrong, it was scary to look in the mirror and see the real me, painful to think that was part of me, waking up to see the shadows and the dark sides of me.

I realised it was no picnic, unravelling my thoughts and feelings, seeing the behaviours I had demonstrated in the past. I had become consciously aware, tapping into deep unfamiliar feelings, and shining a bright light on my vulnerabilities and the patterns that were now exposed. I knew I had to feel them to heal them, and that would take time.

My inner, critical, familiar voice took the driver's seat, reminding me of 'not being good enough'. Anxiety, anger, stress, and doubt all re-surfaced. I wanted to run away but I continued and stayed tuned in.

At the beginning, to avoid these painful feelings and emotions, I reverted to my default familiar behaviour patterns from the past: self-medicating with alcohol. However, this time it didn't work, and I could see something different in me. I hurt like a mirror smashed into a million small pieces, everywhere I looked the small parts stared back at me.

In those counselling sessions, so many things came up for me... around the way I saw myself, my thoughts about relationships, and my family. One of the big ones was the realisation that the only way I had ever been able to relax was by using alcohol to help me. To be honest, feeling anything was completely new in itself, you see prior to the counselling, I'd just felt either numb or angry most of the time, with a small opening of light now and again.

The New Medication – Meditation

I didn't, at that point, have a way to process all these new discoveries and at times the feelings were overwhelming...

That's when I discovered a local meditation group and decided to give it a go. It was cheaper than buying bottles of wine and would hopefully offer a more positive outcome than the hangovers I had recently suffered.

The following week I attended one of the weekly meditation meetings that took place in a large Victorian house that had been turned into a community space. The house was positioned on top of a hill on the edge of a small village.

I remember it was raining heavily that night. I arrived alone for my first session and the car park was dimly lit. I was shaking and feeling very unsure about the situation but I had made the effort, so I had to give it a go and go in. I walked into the house and followed the sign to the meditation room. Once inside the room there were a dozen or more people standing around with cups of tea chatting.

An elderly gentleman, resembling what I can only describe as a wizard, with a white wispy beard and matching hair, approached me and introduced himself as the meditation tutor. He asked if I had ever experienced any meditation previously and after I answered saying I was quite a novice, he went on to explain how the guided meditation session in this group would unfold.

Ten minutes later, I'd joined the group, sitting in a large circle. In the centre of the circle was the largest amethyst crystal I have ever seen.

The tutor closed the door and turned the lights off. It went very dark as he took his seat and set the music to play. Following his instructions, I closed my eyes and started to listen to his voice guiding the meditation. This was a new experience for me and I started to relax, deeper and deeper, it felt so nice, so relaxing, just drifting, until suddenly, out of the blue, a sudden rush of panic erupted inside me. I didn't feel comfortable. My mind started to race. My familiar inner critical voice stirred from within, then the unfolding of an inner dialogue, story, and questions.

Who are these people?

What if these people are not safe?

I don't know anyone here, they could attack me.

I began to feel panic set in, and I looked around for an escape. Peeping through half-closed eyes, I noticed everyone still had their eyes closed. I tried to see in the darkness of the room, thinking to myself *can I locate that door I arrived through earlier?* The door was now behind me and I screwed up my eyes, trying to focus as I looked for it over my shoulder. I could just make out a small night light that highlighted the sign in bold letters: EXIT.

I felt an overwhelming urgency to get up and run out of the door, my heart had started beating so fast it felt like I was having a heart attack.

I tried to reason with my mind: *these people will think I'm stupid running away. I can't. Or can I?*

At that very moment, I closed my eyes, took a deep breath and got ready to run. And then the most amazing experience happened to me.

Starting from just above the crown chakra of my head, moving down to the centre of my forehead, my third eye, in that space between my eyes, came a vision so wonderful, a beautiful bright white dove, wings half folding, bringing me peace and the most amazing *feelings* of calmness. This calmness consumed every cell of my body and lasted only seconds but changed how I *felt* then in that moment and forever. This experience I will always remember forever, and I now know why the dove is the sign of peace. I had experienced it firsthand that evening.

This was a further sign along my path to becoming me, it felt so right, and I wanted more of it. It was addictive. It was my new medication, and it was free.

From that day forward, I knew I would never be afraid or panic and want to run away ever again. I had suddenly realised that not facing things and being invisible was something I'd done all my life.

I decided it was time to let go and stop running away. Since then, I have trusted this calm, peaceful, feeling that meditation gives me. It is a gift that provides clarity and power from within me to meet challenges that come up in my life that I can approach and resolve with a different energy.

My meetings at the house on the hill became a weekly ritual and my spiritual path opened and expanded to a higher energy of calmness more and more.

This inner guidance showed me the way to be and how to work, responding to every client I worked with in a focused pure energy. Seeing each unique person's pain in a different way.

My eyes had been opened, I could see energy around me, connect to deeper levels within people, it was like a new language I could read without words. A soul reader in action, I had tapped into my inner power, allowing it to guide me, and I trusted its communication that I shared more and more with the world.

Takeaway Lesson

The decision to step out of my comfort zone and explore meditation that day changed everything. What I discovered was that meditation isn't about sitting cross-legged and chanting – it's about creating space within yourself to connect with your inner strength and wisdom.

It's a practice that calms the mind, soothes the spirit, and empowers you to meet life's challenges with a sense of clarity and peace.

Meditation taught me that I didn't need to run any more, instead, I could face whatever came my way with a deep inner calm that was always there, waiting for me to tap into it.

By simply committing to stillness, you can unlock a higher level of consciousness, where inner peace and personal growth naturally follow.

Chapter Eleven
Repeating Old Patterns One Last Time

As a newly qualified counsellor, I decided to start my own wellbeing groups. I set them up in my local community to support people with stress and called my group 'Coping with Stress in a Positive Way'. I secured a community grant from the Millennium Fund, which enabled me to find community space to provide a safe space to connect with people.

Each session we would share stories, and I would provide a weekly takeaway tool to try out, that I had used on my journey, to build resilience and reduce stress in their own life. During that time, I had the pleasure of meeting and working with a group of wonderful people and witnessed the positive transformational changes they made in their own lives.

They eagerly tried the tools I provided, enriching their personal growth and my growth in return.

I felt I had found my purpose and was in tune when counselling or coaching. I knew because it gave me a deep sense of happiness and positive energy from within.

I started to see the manifestations of my goals into reality. My life flowed and I felt content in my work – which also rewarded me with financial abundance and security.

But there was one area of my life out of balance, something was missing and that was someone to share my experiences with, a loving partner. Maybe it was time to start looking for someone new.

That someone new showed up in my life two months later. Looking back, I don't think it mattered how I felt about the relationship as I just needed the attention to feel worthy, a new man in my life. I guess I was lonely.

I always went for the same type of man. They usually turned out to be a narcissist, but on first meeting I would be attracted to them because of familiar physical traits of past relationships.

They reminded me of the past and good times in relationships in the early getting-to-know-each-other stage.

My chosen partners were always someone else's leftovers who didn't understand them. For me, on first meeting a new/old, recycled relationship, it seemed to feed my addictive trait and tap into my comfort zone of people-pleasing and rescuing.

This was an obvious default pattern in my life that needed to be worked on, a lesson I needed to learn and complete, and little did I know at the time, that was about to begin.

This new man I will call Dave, recently divorced and living back at his parents' house. Dave had an air of confidence and calmness about him, I wanted more of this calmness in my life and relationships, I remember thinking to myself maybe we could meditate together.

After a few months, Dave moved in with me.

I tried to maintain my independence by charging Dave rent, treating him more like a 'roommate' than a partner. But each time he took the money back, promising to pay it later, I felt a quiet sense of defeat. It was as if, with every broken promise, I was losing pieces of myself, yet I stayed – justifying it all as part of being in a relationship.

Looking back, I realise that we were simply tolerating each other, both using the relationship to fill voids that went far deeper than either of us wanted to admit.

For me, the relationship wasn't about love – it was about filling the emptiness I felt inside, trying to fit the image I thought others expected of me. I had ticked the box of being in a relationship, but deep down I knew it wasn't real, not for him and not for me. Meanwhile, he enjoyed the comfort of living in my home, free from the responsibilities of contributing financially or even stepping up as a father figure to my son. We were both stuck, getting our needs met in superficial ways, but at the cost of something deeper and more meaningful.

My focus was always being protective and making sure Ben's happiness came first, and then my new coaching groups.

Little did I know my life was about to take yet another unexpected turn. In a single day, everything changed course, sending me on a detour I hadn't planned but was curious enough to explore.

City Builders Get Firsthand Care

It was early spring in 2004, and as I waited to begin my coaching session, a small advert in the local free paper caught my eye: *"Wellbeing Professional Required for Construction Company."* It was so specific, so random, yet somehow, it spoke to me. My intuition kicked in, and before I knew it, I was dialling the number. One thing led to another, and I was invited for an interview the next day. I figured, why not see what this is all about?

The next morning, I found myself in the heart of Manchester, about to meet two women who had driven four hours down from Scotland just to interview me. Everything was moving at lightning speed. The setting was surreal – an informal chat at a hotel restaurant, where the two of them leisurely enjoyed a three-course lunch, while I nervously clung to my glass of water, hoping my dry mouth wouldn't betray me. It felt like something out of a strange dream, or maybe an odd TV show – two women eating their desserts, asking me about my coaching experience, while I sipped water and tried to stay composed.

Just when I thought I'd misread the whole situation, they offered me the job: a Wellbeing Advisor for construction workers. Occupational Health Advisor, they said. "But wait, I'm not trained in Occupational Health," I blurted, suddenly unsure if this was all a mistake.

"Don't worry," they reassured me, "you're a qualified nurse, and your counselling and coaching skills are exactly what we need. Plus, we'll cover the cost of your Occupational Health training."

And just like that, my unexpected detour had turned into a brand new adventure.

It seemed so exciting and easy. This experience had manifested and unfolded with flow. I accepted the role, it *felt* intuitively right, and I went to work in a very predominately male-orientated construction site environment. I loved it, there was so much energy and activity. I felt so alive.

Being in this new environment, I realised I had the opportunity to apply my skills in a completely different way. Instead of treating illnesses or managing psychological injuries after they occurred, as I had done in the NHS, I could focus on prevention – helping people stay healthy before they reached a breaking point. It felt empowering to shift from curing to preventing, knowing I could make a real difference in people's lives by addressing their wellbeing proactively.

I remember stepping into my on-site office for the first time, clutching my trusted crystals and daily journal, and feeling an unexpected sense of calm. Life felt good, and I was settling into this newfound energy. It was refreshing to be in a place where I could use my skills with such a diverse group – people from all walks of life in the construction industry. Slowly but surely, I began introducing the benefits of meditation over medication, encouraging physical and mental wellbeing. Sure, the big, burly builders sometimes laughed, but I could tell they were intrigued. Meeting them, hearing their stories, and learning about their unique lifestyles and skill sets was fascinating. It was like entering a whole new world, and I felt excited about the possibilities.

I got to know how buildings were designed, planned, then created and, of course, the dangers involved when constructing the building, and the safety measurements required to keep workers safe.

After accepting the role, both my profile and the company's reputation soared. They proudly positioned themselves as one of the first construction companies to employ a full-time nurse and wellbeing expert on-site, highlighting their commitment to their employees' overall wellbeing. Assessing fitness for work in such a challenging, high-risk environment felt groundbreaking, and the local newspaper even featured me on the front page – there I was, bandaging a colleague's injured hand. It was more than just First Aid; it was a public statement that this company was serious about protecting its workers' health and safety. The image sent a strong message to the community: here was a company willing to invest in its people, making sure everyone went home safe after a hard day on the building site.

Unfortunately, a year later I witnessed the impact of these high-risk dangers firsthand whilst working in this environment. On a nearby project, a major accident resulted in a worker losing his life and the impact on those left behind, their family, loved ones and work colleagues who witnessed the event, was traumatic for all involved.

I attended the project where the accident had occurred the following day. The atmosphere and energy felt so heavy, it was as if you could almost feel death and an eery silence remained, the only talking and conversations were when answering questions asked by the police and the HSE (Health and Safety Executive) visitors who arrived during the tough days and weeks that followed.

My job role was to be visible, listen to, support, coach and guide and I was ready to be seen. My aim was to assist these workers in the healing process from this trauma and pain. Unravelling their numbness, anxiety and depression that had started to develop, trapped in layers of emotions and feelings too fearful for words to explain.

I witnessed familiar patterns: workers leaving work early to escape, running away from the pain, a pain that remained and that followed them home or to the pub. It didn't go away, it returned the next day. I set up a quiet confidential room where I listened and held a safe space for their feelings and emotions to unfold. I witnessed the outbursts of anger, guilt, shame, and pain that all played out in this group of men who wanted to try to express their pain or hide feelings of shame.

I could see and feel the energy that seeped through their faces and was highlighted in their body language as they tried to hide their eyes. They wrestled to stay in control and didn't want to show any vulnerability or be exposed – as 'men don't cry'.

I stayed centred like a large rock in a storm; I felt comfortable with emotions. I had come to know these familiar signs so well myself, my own old negative thought patterns revisited. But this time I noticed them in someone else sitting directly in front of me, they were not my own. I guided them by sharing ideas and offering them practical ways to look after their physical and mental wellbeing.

Post Traumatic Stress Disorder (PTSD), disturbed sleep, anxiety, lacking focus, these were the major culprits surfacing and imprisoning people in pain, and that required a presence to listen.

Over the following days, weeks and months that followed, the emotional storm eased and my relationship with this group of workmen grew stronger as the trust gradually built. Healing started to appear. The workplace atmosphere and energy loosened and became lighter, and their resilience grew over the following year. This became my new family. A bond had been formed and my journey for the next seven years would be spent working in and alongside these sensitive yet tough workers in the construction industry.

Over the seven years, this work took me to a variety of different projects where I supported familiar faces on different sites. The same workers travelled to each new project, along with me, their wellbeing coach, nurse and advisor. I grew more into ME and my identity, along with the buildings that grew to be landmarks of Manchester City Centre, changing the skylines of the city. These buildings remain monuments and memories of my life and time working in the construction industry.

Takeaway Lesson

My time on the building site became a powerful metaphor for my life's journey. Just as constructing a building requires vision, patience, and relentless effort, so does the process of personal transformation. Every great structure begins as a blueprint in the mind, and every goal is built brick by brick, decision by decision. Over time, the once-distant vision slowly takes shape and becomes reality.

Life, much like architecture, presents us with choices, whether to craft it in vibrant colour or let it remain in muted shades of grey. It's the small, seemingly insignificant tasks, done consistently and with intention every day, that lay the foundation for lasting change. With the right tools – discipline, focus, and the right mindset – any dream can be designed, built, and achieved.

Chapter Twelve
Lessons in Love

Throughout my journey, you have probably noticed a theme: always wanting to focus and heal other people's pain. This, my passion and purpose, allowed me to feel alive and in flow, and I once more started to feel stronger internal connections to grow.

However, that energy flow became ignored and restricted when it came to my personal relationships which I chose to attract by looking for love in all the wrong places, with all the wrong people, and never quite finding it for myself.

The day came when this lesson finally had to be learned. Leaving me to deal with final endings. These were initially overwhelming and distressing, but in time would start to heal that part of me that had been missing and allow inner growth to heal me.

Within a two-month time span, all my close male relationships changed.

My life was about to unfold and fall apart and I could not turn and run away. It was time for me to discover a long-held limiting belief within me and see it challenged, activating my biggest healing and setting me free.

Up until that moment, I am sure you can gather I had always felt lonely and unloved. I believed that to fit in, I needed to be in a relationship. But in this area of my life, I didn't know who I was or how I should be.

My Achilles' heel had always been my inability to love myself or accept love from others. Deep down, I felt a constant emptiness. The only love I truly knew was the love I felt for my son, Ben – it was the one love that flowed effortlessly. But when it came to loving myself or believing I deserved love from others, I was lost. I questioned whether I was ever good enough to be loved and often pushed partners away before they had the chance to reject me.

In 2006, this painful lesson was brought to the surface in the hardest way possible. One by one, all my close male relationships were tested and fell apart. It was then that I realised love was a lesson I couldn't avoid any longer.

This was the year that my dad was diagnosed with terminal bowel cancer. The man who had always been in my life, always there for me and my son. My dad, my rock, the one stable, male, role model I loved, and who had shaped Ben's life growing up. Ben loved and respected him deeply. He just couldn't leave me.

Ben was now sixteen years old and leaving school. With the news about his grandad, he suddenly changed – he developed a bad attitude overnight. He stopped talking to me and I was heartbroken. What had I done wrong? Ben decided he was grown up enough to leave home, move out and live at my sister's house with his older cousin.

I felt lost, anxiety starting to tap into my feelings that grew stronger and visibly surfaced outwardly, I withdrew, went back into distractions, focused on work.

I needed support, to make sense of what was happening in my life.

Plucking up the courage, I lowered my guard. Wanting to trust, I shared my vulnerability, distress and upset with my partner, who immediately dismissed my feelings, rejected me and confirmed what I expected would happen.

He failed to give me any emotional support or understanding. He was detached from any empathy and was only concerned about his own needs in all this chaos.

Once again, I felt abandoned and lost.

I immediately slipped back into old belief patterns, despite my newfound awareness and intuition. It felt easier to just keep it all inside and not share, he just didn't want to know or try to understand, and this lack of support in times of great need highlighted it to me and I just didn't know where to turn.

Deciding not to do anything, I just waited for Ben to need me and call. He had always been a talented footballer and lived to play the game. However, now all he wanted to do was be free, drinking alcohol with his new friends and even playing football while drunk.

A few months passed, and then the call I was waiting for came. One night, Ben had been playing football and had broken his leg. I rushed to meet the ambulance at the local A&E with my reluctant partner. Sitting in the waiting room I could hear Ben's screams from the emergency room as they tried multiple times to reset his leg. Both bones had been broken in his lower right leg. Unable to reset his leg with only gas and air sedation, he was listed for surgery that evening.

The following day my partner remained distant towards me, no regular morning calls on my way to work or lunchtime like he normally did to check up on me. It felt odd, after all, he liked to control me and know where I was at all times.

I carried on with my day and in the evening, I went to see Ben. He was still drowsy, and due to the lack of beds on the orthopaedic ward, he had been placed on the colorectal surgical ward.

I remember feeling alarmed and thinking that this was not good at all: to be placed on this ward after having this type of surgery could cause cross-infection.

My stress levels were on high alert and anxiety kicked in even more as I noticed bleeding coming from the bottom of Ben's white plaster cast. I called the nurse who didn't seem worried about what she witnessed, however, she told me her speciality was related to bowel surgery and the care and routines of the colorectal surgical patients. I asked her how could she advise on a patient's orthopaedic post-op care. She told me the bleeding would probably stop by elevating Ben's leg – which she did.

I stayed and watched as Ben's pain started to build and increased at speed. There was something wrong.

My intuition continued to shout at me, my feelings intensified, something was not right. Trying to remain calm, I went back in my mind remembering my nurse training and times spent on the orthopaedic wards. I called the nurse back again and demanded to see an orthopaedic doctor. Reluctantly, after several requests and eventually threatening to take action and make a complaint about her if she didn't call him, she called the orthopaedic doctor. He eventually arrived two hours later.

"You need to cut this cast off," I demanded.

The orthopaedic doctor looked disapprovingly at me as I continued.

"I can't feel any foot pulses," I said, "can you?" The doctor then tried to locate the foot pulse and wasn't sure if he could feel it or not.

I intuitively knew that Ben was developing compartment syndrome (bleeding and swelling within the enclosed muscle, restricting blood flow to the muscle and nerves that then start to die).

The doctor reluctantly followed my request, and the plaster was cut away. The blood escaped, absorbing into and filling the white sheets, and turning them bright red. Ben was now losing large amounts of blood and the colour in his face drained away as he went quickly into shock. The doctor looked at me in disbelief at what he had just witnessed as he quickly made decisions about what to do next. He instructed the nurse to call the theatre and listed Ben for urgent surgery.

Ben was rushed back into surgery that evening and the following day, before continuing his treatment, he required two blood transfusions.

Ben's leg had been cut from his ankle to his knee to release the pressure and save the internal muscle. He had to undergo a further five operations, going into theatre every other day over the following weeks to stitch small amounts of muscle and tissue back into place to allow his leg muscle to fully recover and ultimately survive. I had followed my inner guidance and trusted my feelings, I was glad I did speak up and challenged myself. I had saved Ben's leg.

Takeaway Lesson

Sometimes we can give our power away, believing that our inner guidance is not correct. I doubted my feelings throughout this challenging time, told by these trained professionals they knew best. Even my own family doubted me, however, I had background knowledge and training in this area, and I knew deep inside – that gut feeling – something was not right.

My determination and will to be guided by those feelings gave me the power to step forward and confirm I was right.

I now appreciated the time that I had spent working those long agency shifts, learning on the job, needing to know how and what to do with complicated fractures on the orthopaedic wards. This had paid off and served me well, along with listening to my inner guidance and following it through. I had retained this information for a reason – not knowing that one day it would save my own son's leg.

The Lessons in Love Continued

Three weeks later Ben returned home. Learning to use crutches and unable to run away, he relied on me now in every way. I felt this was meant to be: to bring him back home safe to me.

Ben continued to improve every day and used the crutches less and less after intense physio appointments. I needed to pay the bills and had to go to work when it was time for his six-week check-up. He assured me he would be fine without me there – all he wanted to ask the consultant was when he could play football again. That day the consultant's answer to this question smashed Ben's dreams into pieces and left him overwhelmed with grief and loss. He could not believe that his life would not include playing football again.

Arriving back home and hearing this news I felt his deep pain as if it was my own. It was then, in that moment, the first time he connected and believed what I was about to tell him. I looked at him, holding eye contact as I told him, "Don't let anyone tell you what you can and can't do, only you get to decide if it is true for you." He decided there and then what would be his truth.

The following month Ben gingerly stepped back onto the football pitch, overcoming his fears and setting himself free. He has continued to play, scoring goals on the pitch, fully fit, and still playing even years later.

I am a proud mum witnessing her son overcoming fear and having belief, courage and faith in creating what he desired.

As I have mentioned earlier, always trust and be guided from within, without listening to the normal old stories on repeat of doubts or fears blocks that are within.

Answers and guidance will always appear when you go within. Speaking up for yourself is not easy and so often we ignore our 'self', our own power within.

Our intuition is never wrong. Choosing your intuition is the same as choosing truth, but there are times when the messages seem unclear, you're not sure it's right, or you just don't feel ready. Trust and take action even if you hesitate because of fear of change, that too, is reflective of some part of your emotional truth. Look at where the conflict lies and take some time to consider all factors.

Back at home, my life continued to spiral into total chaos and confusion, I felt numb, my partner chose to keep his distance from me, uninterested in what I was going through with Ben and my dad's prognosis. Too exhausted to argue, I carried on and left him alone to do his own thing. Weeks passed and we became more and more detached.

I started to pay attention. I noticed my partner had changed even more, every evening after finishing work he made it a regular routine to bring home alcohol. We normally never had drinks in the house and now, on work nights, he was drinking bottles of wine and trying to encourage me to join him. I remember thinking he must want to sort things out, even though he had stopped the normal routines of texting or calling me each morning when I left for work. Recently I had felt guilty and started to call him, yet when I did, he seemed distant, saying he was too busy to talk and quickly ending the call. I didn't give this too much attention and thought maybe I was taking away the control he wanted to have by making the calls, so I let it go, my energy was needed elsewhere to get through each working day.

One Saturday afternoon, after visiting my dad in hospital, I arrived home later than normal and noticed my partner's coat hanging on the entrance hall bannister at the bottom of the stairs. As I walked past the coat I smelt it, asking myself why did I just do that? I wasn't sure, couldn't answer my own question, and carried on into the room where he was sitting reading a book.

He glanced up. "Do you want a cup of tea?" I asked. He nodded.

I went into the kitchen and standing at the sink, I felt a sudden thought flash into my mind and an urge to go and ask him a question. Without knowing why I was asking it, and with no feelings attached to what I was thinking, I went into the living room and said, "If I ask you a question will you tell me the truth?"

He looked up irritated and said, "Yes, what is it?"

I said, "Are you seeing someone else?"

He looked surprised and quickly said, "No."

I casually said, "Okay," and carried on making the drinks, not thinking of why I had asked him such a random and unexpected question.

The distance between us continued. We were spending time in the house, sleeping in the same bed yet not together, and after work when we arrived home we didn't spend long in the same room.

One evening he arrived home with yet another bottle of wine.

"Have a drink with me," he said.

I reluctantly agreed this time (he constantly asked every time he came back with wine). After a few drinks I loosened up and mentioned to him my feelings about how he had seemed distant over the last few months and maybe I had been distant also. He wanted to move away from the questions and tried to close the conversation down saying he didn't know why and wanted to relax, enjoy the evening, change the subject. So we did – after we both agreed to start making more of an effort with time for each other going forward.

I felt lighter having discussed my concerns, and feeling very drunk, I went to bed, leaving him to finish drinking. After falling asleep, I suddenly woke up, I could hear talking. I looked across to his side of the bed. He wasn't there. I walked quietly to the top of the stairs. I could hear him talking on the phone.

I heard the words "I miss you so much" and "I can't wait to see you."

My heart started to race as I ran down the stairs, he quickly put the phone handset down. "Who was on the phone?" I shouted at him abruptly, demanding answers.

"It's my brother," he replied.

"I don't believe you, call him back," I shouted.

He refused. I felt rage and anger bubble up, I couldn't believe it. I went back upstairs trying to calm down and work out what to do next.

Moments later, to my disbelief, I could hear him back on the phone. I ran down the stairs once more and unplugged the landline from the wall socket. He laughed at me, picking up his mobile phone and walking out into the back garden. My anger turned to tears and I felt my heart break. I had been used and rejected once more. Looking back, I realise I needed to have someone, anyone, to fill the gap of loneliness that I felt inside and that came with consequences and lessons to learn!

That experience highlighted my neediness and trying to fill a gap in my life. I know now that the work that was required was the inner work to find me.

This was all about to change.

The following morning, we both got up and went to work without speaking.

Luckily, Ben had a sleepover that night at Stee's house so missed all the drama of the night.

Arriving home from work that evening, followed shortly after by my partner, I asked him if I could have a word with him. He followed me upstairs where I'd already packed his belongings. I told him to leave.

"You are never coming back from this," I said.

He just looked at me with a blank expression on his face, took the bag and left the house.

I felt mixed emotions, regret of wasted years spent with this person who I had allowed into my family life. I became angry about another failed relationship that added to the pile of mistakes and lack, once more the familiar internal voice confirming I was not worthy to be loved.

Having very little sleep that night, I arrived at work the following morning trying my best not to be seen. It didn't work! My name was called out and I was suddenly visible. My good friend and colleague, the safety manager, approached me, immediately noticing something was wrong. Maybe it was the dark circles under my eyes that gave the game away!

He followed me into my office and sat down. I felt uncomfortable with a feeling of being very exposed and vulnerable. I walked outside onto the viewing platform, watching the scaffolders scaling the outside of the new building.

"What's happened?" he asked. "I can tell by your eyes something is wrong."

The windows of my soul had exposed me. I remained focused, staring at the building directly in front, keeping strong and trying extremely hard not to cry.

My voice started shaking as I spoke, sharing the drama that had unfolded the night before.

That day the Universe/God/this bigger presence that is always present in all of us (yes, always present), sent me this very person to be at my side, to listen, hold space and care.

We stood side by side as he listened, looked at me and then back at the building in front of us. After listening to the full story unfold, he turned to me and said, "Anyone on this building site would sincerely want to support you and be there for you, these guys think the world of you, you are more than just the nurse, you make a massive difference here, just by being you."

Those words – the feedback that I was making an impact, that people cared about ME – felt so heart-warming and sincere. Something in that very moment clicked deep inside, I had listened and heard feedback that people liked me for the first time in my life. I believed it was true, I gained the strength in myself that day that I needed to carry on. Work once again gave me comfort and my inner mindset changed, moving up a gear that very day.

Takeaway Lesson

Loneliness can be felt in a room full of people and that's how I felt most of my life: abandoned, rejected and alone, not lovable up until that day that changed me. A gift had been given, finding the biggest part of ME that had been missing all my life's journey until now, it had always been inside waiting to be called forward in full power to serve.

My three relationships changed:

1. **Ending the relationship with my partner:** I finally realised I wouldn't settle for less than I deserved in a partner. For too long, I ignored my gut, burying my intuition

just to keep the relationship going. That was dangerous because when you silence your inner voice in one area of your life, it becomes harder to hear it elsewhere. While I don't regret taking the time I needed, the moment I chose to listen, my life started to improve in ways I couldn't have imagined.

2. **Growing up with Ben:** Ben faced a life-changing challenge when doctors said he'd never play football again. I told him to believe in himself, and he did. He not only played again but scored goal after goal. This journey brought us closer, and it taught us both the power of trusting our inner guidance.

3. **Losing my dad:** The hardest lesson was losing my dad far too soon. Even though he's no longer physically here, I feel his presence with me, guiding me from beyond. I find peace in knowing he watches over me, always nearby in spirit.

Chapter Thirteen
The Growing Years

My dad was cremated and laid to rest.

Now fully recovered and back playing football, Ben and I grew closer as it was just the two of us together. He found a suitable job role on the construction site where I worked which meant we worked together too. Then Ben passed his driving test and started driving for a construction company. Life flowed. We celebrated Ben's eighteenth birthday together in Spain on an all-inclusive holiday where we had a magical time and made lasting memories to treasure forever. I knew he would probably not want to go away with his mum again after this holiday.

I felt it was time to focus on myself. I started a new business again – providing wellbeing for the up-and-coming new construction sites that had been set up to start new building work in and around Manchester.

Each new building completed provided me with a lasting memory, a stage in my life showing how far I had come along my journey of transformational change. I had started to like and care about myself, and I liked who I was becoming. I tuned in to my deep intuitive connection more and more, and this felt like an electrical current of inner power, I felt energised, alive, finally getting to know the real me. This new relationship with myself was the best. I had connected to the feelings within using them as my satnav, writing endless pages, journaling about energy, intuition, and spirit guidance that flowed from my pen onto the paper in front of me, an outlet for this magical energy bubbling up inside me.

This motivated and assisted me in my own daily life. For the first time in my life, I was me, happy, confident and free without any restrictions, choosing when and where to be. I had taken control of my life and was creating what I liked.

After the holiday, I returned home and went to work on the biggest building contract at the time in Manchester. This project required two thousand construction workers and a team of nurses.

Being self-employed, I worked on the project part-time and expanded my knowledge by becoming interested in further training as a hypnotherapist. I had the freedom to be creative in my wellbeing role on the construction site, wanting to add something new to the wellbeing clinics provided on site. Hypnotherapy seemed like a good fit; I had the ideal clients, a plethora of construction workers.

After obtaining consent from management to offer the hypnotherapy service, I set about advertising around the site. I set to work offering free sessions to volunteers who wanted to experience hypnotherapy, working on a variety of issues such as giving up smoking, drinking, gambling, weight loss, changing mindsets and improving work morale. My hypnotherapy sessions became very popular, and I refined my skills and techniques whilst providing an extra beneficial service for free.

The General Wellbeing Clinics, run separately, had the regular visitors, and this is where I met my new partner, Tony. I wasn't looking for a partner and neither was he. I no longer needed to be in a relationship or be with someone to feel loved and secure, however, the Universe had different ideas and aligned our paths to meet, placing us together.

Tony worked in the offices on the construction site and visited the clinic for a weekly blood pressure check. He had had a second kidney transplant ten years previously and needed to keep a close eye on his blood pressure levels.

I started noticing that every time he arrived at the clinic, I would suddenly change. Physically, a surge of energy, excitement and laughter took over me. I would talk nonstop while he remained calm, seriously trying to focus and to get the best blood pressure levels for his records. Each time he left the clinic, I noticed my energy settle and return to normal, leaving me with a lasting feeling of happiness inside. I noticed he was changing my energy and blood pressure!

Over the months that followed, I got to know more and more about Tony's personal life as he shared snippets on the weekly clinic visits. He was recently divorced and had two young daughters. He was a loving dad who valued the weekends and time with his girls, and always seemed happier on the weekends when it was his turn to have them come over and stay with him.

This wonderful man had stirred something new in me, a feeling like no other, I didn't know what it could be. All I knew was I felt good being in his company. A few months passed and one day, whilst visiting the clinic, Tony asked me out for a drink. I agreed without hesitation. The relationship gradually grew over time. Tony was different, so romantic and patient, this type of relationship was very new to me. We enjoyed travelling and new adventures together and within a couple of years my family had expanded to include two beautiful stepdaughters. A new happy chapter began in my life, a relationship that felt right in every way. We set up home together, making lasting memories.

After being together for ten years, Tony started to feel unwell and slowly went into kidney failure – after having the donor kidney for nearly twenty years. He required kidney dialysis every other day to keep him alive whilst waiting for a third kidney transplant.

This changed our lifestyle. I loved this man so much and we decided to commit and get married before he started dialysis treatment so we could all share a perfect day. We had a small wedding with just the close family of Ben and the girls to witness our happy occasion, in one of our favourite places in the UK, Anglesey.

After getting married, Tony returned home and started his treatment.

He had his dialysis treatment at the local hospital unit. Every other day, for six hours each session, he had needles attached to his arm that allowed tubes to enter his body to remove blood that was then pumped into a machine to wash out all the impurities – completing that job that his kidneys could no longer manage to do.

Takeaway Lesson

Life often presents challenges that test our strength and adaptability, and living with someone who faces daily health battles can reshape your perspective on love, resilience, and gratitude. Watching Tony manage his dialysis with such grace, while still making time to work and prioritise my happiness, filled me with a deep sense of admiration and respect.

This experience taught me that love isn't just about the easy moments, it's about supporting each other through the hard ones and finding joy in the time you do have together. No matter the limitations life places on us, it's how we choose to face them that truly defines the strength of our relationships.

Chapter Fourteen
Adventures in Hypnotherapy

After the final big build in the Manchester project, it was decision time for me. The next new projects would mean travelling or relocating to London. I had to make that decision fast. I knew what that decision would be: to stay at home with Tony. We already had restrictions on our time together without me travelling up and down the country.

It seemed to be the right time to move on from the construction work and try something new. After seeing the results with the people on the construction site using hypnosis – many stopping smoking, losing weight, or reducing stress levels – I had good research and evidence that I could achieve lasting results. This gave me the belief and confidence to set up a hypnotherapy business, a new adventure and tools to use now that I had qualified.

Months later, I finally felt ready, fully aligned with my intuition and eager to take the next step. I rented a room in a local office building, feeling the excitement of starting something new.

Not long after settling in, I crossed paths with Anne, another therapist who had specialised in addiction. She had spent years working at some of the most renowned addiction centres but had recently taken the leap to work independently. Her experience was impressive, and I could sense immediately that meeting her would be significant. It felt like the Universe was weaving together the connections I needed at just the right time.

Her room was at the top of the office building next door to me. I felt very new to this world of therapy in such professional settings and in the early days felt like an imposter in the environment that I now found myself in.

After a couple of months getting to know each other, I realised Anne and I had a lot in common and we became good friends. We decided it would be more economical to share office space, especially as Anne only worked two days per week, so this arrangement benefited both of our needs.

We shared a deep spiritual connection and had very similar energy that blended well in the room we had started to share. Over the next few years, Anne became a very good friend, and we spent social time celebrating birthdays and Christmas times together.

My client list grew along with my skills and confidence. I enjoyed meeting a variety of clients, creating deep connections with each one, witnessing many clients transform and have their own unique journeys, and experiencing 'penny drop' moments that lit up their faces and brought the room alive with energy – all confirming that this is where I was meant to be. My business steadily grew and I was becoming well known, with very successful outcomes, always a full clinic and even a waiting list.

It was around this time I noticed Anne had been unwell for some months in that year. She had a bad chest infection and a terrible cough that wouldn't go away. I'd hear her cough before she got to the office door on the days she was at work. I pushed and pushed for her to see the GP and reluctantly, after some persuasion, she went. The GP gave her yet another course of antibiotics and arranged for an X-ray.

Two weeks later, after getting the results from her X-ray, she was still in shock as she broke the news to me. She had been diagnosed with terminal lung cancer. I couldn't believe it, we both sat in silence for what seemed like hours, trying to process this terrible, upsetting news.

Anne lived alone, was in her early 60s, and refused to have any treatment for her condition, including an operation to remove the infected lung. She was a fiercely independent woman who didn't want to suffer post-operatively in pain, and who would require oxygen and someone else to be there to care and look after her.

Being self-employed and with her client work as her only form of income, Anne decided that whilst she felt well enough, she would continue to practise.

The winter arrived and Anne's chest became infected once more. This time I noticed she was becoming breathless and blue tinges appeared around her lips even when sitting down. She decided it was time to give up her work.

I couldn't believe what I witnessed, she seemed so active and full of life. She had always had a good lifestyle – other than smoking cigarettes, which I might add, she continued to do despite being told to give up. I felt so helpless, wanting to help. I offered her sessions in hypnotherapy to help her give up smoking and give her mind and body a chance to heal. She refused, she enjoyed smoking and didn't want to give up her only addiction/vice.

I tried to persuade her, to change her mind to have some form of treatment, but she had made up her mind and nobody could change it. I had to accept her decision and realised I could not force her to change until she was ready to change, and only she could decide when that would be.

Our friendship continued and I remained in close contact, keeping her up to date with the office changes and life in general. Two months later, Anne decided to sell her home. She had lived close to me but was now going to move to the east side of the city to be near her sister.

This, she said, would free up some finances for her to be comfortable and be near family.

I was now working full-time from the office and advertised for someone to share the space and the monthly outgoing bills.

Not long after her move, Anne's sister called with news that Anne had died after going to bed one evening. Her sister said she had discovered Anne in bed the following morning when she had popped in to visit. Her sister went on to tell me that Anne had left her final request in writing before she died, stating she did not want a formal funeral or to have any flowers sent.

To be honest, I wasn't surprised by her decision, but I felt very sad that I didn't get to say a final goodbye to her. I had the privilege of meeting and getting to know this amazing woman, a very private and protective lady, whose purpose was to help others heal even though she didn't allow herself to feel and heal.

During our time working together, Anne had shared such funny stories of happier times, and how she had travelled the world in her younger years. She never found love with anyone or herself but said she had no regrets. Anne had allowed me into her world, and I had been honoured to see her true inner self, beneath the hard-shell exterior of the ego self and the mask she wore and presented to the world, protecting herself from any hurt.

I missed her so much and the office just didn't feel the same. When the annual office contract came up to be renewed, I decided that – without Anne – it was time to move on. It would be easier and safer especially in the winter months to see clients in a designated space in my home.

This new arrangement worked well at the beginning, I could work my diary around housework and shopping, however, over time, as clients increased in numbers and sessions, my energy decreased. Working mostly long evenings, it started to feel like hard work. I was not in flow, I needed change. It was time to let go or I would lose me and not be focused on the client's needs.

Takeaway Lesson

Even when things seem to be going well, it's crucial to pause and check in with yourself. You are the only expert on *you*. It's easy to get caught up in the momentum, thinking you just need to push a little harder or hold on a little longer. But when the balance tips, when work drains your energy and life feels out of sync, that's your cue that it's time to make a change. Real self-care isn't about waiting until you're burnt out to recover; it's about recognising when something no longer serves you and giving yourself permission to adjust. Sometimes, letting go is the most empowering thing you can do for your wellbeing.

By listening to yourself and making those shifts, you're not just preserving your energy – you're honouring your own needs and staying aligned with the life you truly want to live.

Chapter Fifteen
Moving On – Changing Lanes

Early June of the following year, I sat recharging my energy, meditating and asking and waiting for direction. It arrived the very next day. The Universe delivered an 'out of the blue' opportunity as it often did. An email popped into my inbox and caught my eye, an exciting opportunity that resonated within me straight away.

A job opportunity working as a wellbeing advisor on a Smart Motorway project. This involved the workers expanding lanes on the motorway to cope with and control the flow of traffic at busy rush hour times. I applied and the following week went along for the interview and successfully secured the position with ease.

A new personal challenge began out of my comfort zone and into the fast lane of motorway life. It was ironic to be working on a motorway project because since passing my driving test many years ago, I had always had a fear of driving on motorways. Always looking for the 'A' road options, the easy option in my mind and one that was reflected in my life. Somehow keeping myself safe.

I believe the Universe had created this role just for me. I had a blank canvas to set up and run the Occupational Health Wellbeing Unit. So, excited for a new challenge, I arrived for my first day along with my inspirational quotes and crystals to furnish my new office. Creative ideas were flowing and buzzing in my head, I was feeling so alive and looking at ways to connect to my new audience. My role was to complete each worker's specialist medical assessments to certify them fully fit, physically and mentally, to work safely in an ever-changing high-speed motorway environment. This role allowed me the freedom to be flexible within wellbeing, focusing on my passion – mindset and mental health – by providing time to talk and introducing and advocating the benefits of learning meditation. When they were not working on the motorway network, of course!

The job roles on the motorway varied, but all the workers worked in the same environment: high-risk areas on the hard shoulders of the motorway, with speeding traffic passing by only inches away from them. Their jobs involved constantly setting and planning lane closures with rows of plastic traffic cones as the only barrier to keep each worker safe.

I spent the following three years working on this project and connecting with amazing creative people whilst learning something new every day about the motorway environment and the planning that was required to work with and around the fields and Mother Nature. I have fond memories of sharing my days with the lives of the motorway workers. However, all that hard work and time would years later be pulled apart by the government realising that Smart Motorways don't work.

Takeaway Lesson

I stepped out of my comfort zone. I conquered my fear of motorways. I realised that this fear

(False Evidence Appearing Real) had restricted my expansion of myself in the past and prevented me from physically travelling out of my familiar comfort zone on roads, but not any more. I had changed my mind a little more.

The road is a metaphor to show me the way forward, opening me up to be clear in my mind and life's path.

This was my journey to continue to transform, expand and manifest a better version of myself each day and in every way as my confidence grew.

The motorway project was completed in 2017. Next, it was time to change lanes and leave the motorway network behind. I was feeling ready for something new to learn and grow.

Chapter Sixteen
There is No Wrong Decision

It's been said that there is no wrong decision in life, and I believe whatever decision we make, we will always have a lesson to learn and grow from that experience. This is one of the many lessons I had to learn, by deciding to grow in a different work environment. I moved on to this new adventure, transferring my skills into the area of food production, but working in a similar role as their Occupational Health and Wellbeing Advisor.

This move challenged me in a very different way. Looking back, it gave me contrast to find the clarity in where I was travelling to on my own life's path. This new role was working in a smaller organisation with business values which attracted me and aligned with my own values. However, over time it became quite apparent these business values didn't appear to be visible or upheld within the business. People within the organisation merely paid lip service to them and I started to lose my true self.

The next two years I spent working in an environment which rapidly started to feel restrictive. I noticed with each passing day my creativity becoming suffocated and smothered. My energy rapidly depleted in the job role and I missed feeling passionate and energised like I used to feel when I followed my inner truth.

Every day became an effort to motivate myself to turn up; I had to try and protect my energy from the people I worked with daily. I had changed my outlook, felt very different about my work and life, and my light within started to go out!

Refusing to walk away from this challenge, I persevered, chipping away, for some reason willing to sacrifice my own inner guidance and wellbeing which was telling me to re-evaluate my position and move on from the toxic situation that was blocking me. Instead, I continued using all the passion I could muster, pushing on, providing information, and delivering wellbeing presentations on mental health and resilience coaching. This was something that I needed to focus on for my own wellbeing.

I believe time is our most valuable possession, we never know when our time will run out, and every minute can save or change your life and create a new mindset. By continuing and refusing to listen to my feelings at this time, I paid an expensive price. Slipping back into negative energy, this was mirrored in my work environment. I created what I didn't want and had joined the status quo. I felt like a positive battery that had become drained of energy. I gave up.

It reminded me of all the toxic relationships I'd put up with in the past. It appeared that the people I worked with were putting in place restrictions and blocks in every situation and meeting I attended. I felt like I was firefighting each long day and yet I know I played my part in this game, and I wasn't sure why I was allowing myself to do it.

I experienced firsthand stress and anxiety escalate in myself the more I worked in this environment, with the accumulation of heavy negative energy, a killer to my health and wellbeing. Depression took hold in my mind and body. The frustration I felt started to develop inner patterns of anger, which in turn generated physical acidic feelings and emotions. I continued to suffer, refusing to listen to my inner guidance, and continued manifesting further confirmation of lack and deeper depression. I would not let go.

By late 2019, each day I was driving to work I felt my own wellbeing become weak. I was slowly dying inside. Why was I still there? My inner guide/knowing still found the energy within to continually shout at me: *How long are you going to waste TIME? Wake up and move on!* Needing time to heal became real; I had always known my life's purpose was to heal people's pain, yet here I was in the depth of pain myself.

How could I help others when I was choosing to remain in fear and doubt, slipping back into old outdated negative patterns, my inner critical voice in charge telling me to conform with people, to fit in, be the people pleaser? I had tuned in to lower vibrational energy and negativity and I felt I had lost the fight.

However, not for long. I finally mustered up the motivation within, this time aware I had a choice and could change. I wasn't ready to die inside, I was unwilling to surrender and stop growing. It was time to step out of the status quo and challenge the situation, become visible and stop struggling to survive. After all, what did I have to lose? It was time to figure out what I could do differently.

Over the Christmas holiday break, I sat quietly, settling my mind, and becoming clear. I started making plans and working with my inner roadmap, I received direction, my passion to reconnect to the flow and energy deep within my soul. It didn't take long to feel that light connection present itself once more from within, and then move forward to take centre stage. My energy felt lighter, I felt happier again.

This was turning in and tuning into me, a new vision and goal.

My purpose about to unfold.

January 2020, the start of the New Year, it was time for me to make the move. Work remained extremely toxic, however, I mustered up new feelings, focusing on my escape plan to leave this behind and move on, I was on my way to happier days. It felt like the right time to set myself free, set up my own business, give it a go once more, while being flexible in finding ways to attract and support people wanting freedom and change just like me. I knew my message would get to the right people.

Then, just like that, everything changed in the world. It was March 2020 – Coronavirus lockdown – COVID-19.

The world had to change and so did the business I worked in. My escape plan had to be put on the back burner for the time being. I felt trapped, in more ways than one! I now became visible and outwardly focused, it felt like I was in a very toxic marriage I could not leave.

My time was spent in a minefield, assessing the medical histories of each of the employees within the business to determine who was required to shield and isolate from this deadly virus, that was being reported in the news headlines on the hour. We had to prioritise and protect the most vulnerable. All these employees were classed as key workers, still required to be in work to produce the food products and feed the nation whilst in lockdown. Employees who were assessed and categorised as high risk had to stay at home. This caused extra pressure for the business, they now required extra staff and made provisions for temporary agency workers to come and fill in the gaps.

It was a challenging time for all involved, fear caused attitudes to change, empathy took a back seat within the higher management team because now the business and its finances were at risk. Workers wanted to work, and the business wanted to survive. Restricting people from working, protecting their health and well-being, became extremely challenging in the early months of the COVID-19 unfolding. Government guidance advised working from home for office staff and employees who were identified as having underlying risks. It was a great relief when the government supported businesses by offering financial support for workers who couldn't afford to be off work but had no choice. With this support, the stress of the situation lifted slightly.

The remaining workforce dropped into low moods as they tried to juggle all the moving parts of life in this sudden challenging situation. Being in families and bubbles of mixed family dynamics, there was always a crisis or extra problem to work out and solve.

At home, my personal life was challenged and changed. Zoom meetings, phone calls and an avalanche of emails, meant my work/life balance had gone, disappeared overnight, and had seeped into one BIG ball of chaos. Colleagues in the business suddenly became 'medical experts' overnight, trying to follow and more often than not misinterpreting the ongoing changing of government medical guidelines. They took great pleasure in misquoting their findings about the virus, challenging the professional medical advice I had been employed to provide and challenging the recommendations that I'd given to each employee I had assessed. Ultimately, I could see my professional medical opinions and decisions were cherry-picked to meet the survival of the business and not in the interest of the health and wellbeing of the individual employees. These boundaries and my own wellbeing were constantly being well and truly pushed.

By August 2020, I was burnt out and fed up, higher management started to go against the guidance provided, and I asked myself *why am*

I still here? I was struggling and continually cutting off my own self-care and self-esteem.

I continued to push on until finally, in November 2020, I felt totally demoralised and completely out of all resources mentally, emotionally, physically, and spiritually. This was the final BIG sign; it was time to say goodbye and leave this business behind. Like the ingredients that made and shaped the products in the factory, I needed to be where I could rise and grow. It is not easier to fit in while remaining in a restrictive mould, allowing only ONE SHAPE to unfold and conforming to the status quo. It was time to go. I had to move on, or I would die inside, stopping my passion and purpose to thrive and feel alive.

This role rewarded me in my personal growth, taught me valuable lessons about my beliefs, my feelings and self-worth, and was a stepping stone to show me who I would become. We need contrast in life to work on finding clarity and a better life. There is always a choice, it just depends on you to take it and make it something better.

I likened this experience to a bad relationship or bad marriage, I was a loyal partner until the very part of my inner self was in so much pain and emotionally drained, I needed to change and take a leap into the unknown. To practise that I was willing to move on and teach others. Have faith over fear it will become clear!

Takeaway Lesson

If this resonates with you or you feel trapped in some area of your life then ask yourself, where, why or how have you stopped growing in your life? Take time today to write down the area of your life where you feel restricted, the answers will come to you.

Slowly you will start to see patterns reflecting and habits and behaviours that may be keeping you stuck.

(Further information can be found in the Toolbox section)

Chapter Seventeen
My Path from Lockdown to Freedom

Mindset reset

The predicted COVID-19 virus second wave hit the country and we all went back into lockdown for Christmas 2020. Constant drip-feeding news channels informed us of death and despair, updated every hour. It was time to turn the news channels off! Feed a different diet to my mind.

During this time, I became consciously aware of one of my old childhood behaviour patterns that had recently resurfaced. I noticed I had started a new ritual that I repeated each evening whilst watching TV and that ritual was eating large amounts of chocolate. It felt like I needed to fill up some void deep inside, feeding some deep hurt, buried emotion that still required healing.

I tuned in to what I was thinking and asked myself how was I feeling consciously in that moment. Suddenly, I realised that it was the younger version of myself wanting comfort and protection, feeding emotional fear, and hiding, pushing the fear down and keeping me safe. Closing my eyes and connecting to this memory, I revisited my eight-year-old self. I could see, back then, I needed space and peace away from the chaos, arguments and noise of my parents arguing and siblings joining in.

I had been taken back to a memory in my home environment and my unpredictable and often explosive childhood days. In times of conflict and unrest, I'd take myself away to hide, become invisible and escape from the uncomfortable fearful energy.

Sitting alone in one corner of the large bedroom, my eight-year-old self would attempt to push away the pain by secretly eating my way through a large tin of *Quality Street* chocolates, telling myself at the end of the tin I would find comfort and satisfaction, I'd fill the empty void inside and feel better. Eating until the final piece made me so sick.

I never filled the void or ate chocolate again, not until lockdown! Because now the world I witnessed felt like my childhood home. This new insight into my actions and feelings in the 'here and now' moment had dropped into my conscious awareness for me to be present to and understand. I had caught the original root belief and pattern that had caused my repeated behaviour, something deep within me needed attention. My eight-year-old 'self' needed to heal, feel loved and safe in a more nurturing and positive way. Allowing me to have less weight to carry inside and out.

From that moment on I started changing my daily habits and routines. I was aware that an uncluttered body and mind would energise my soul. I started with daily walks in nature, affirming my self-worth and processing my feelings using physical movement and emotional journaling. I snipped away, changing deep-rooted patterns, beliefs and behaviours.

Some of those early days in lockdown were hard, exhausting my energy. Challenging the unwanted patterns that once had been so comfortable and familiar. Feelings of embarrassment and shame came through and I had no one to share with because of my fear they wouldn't understand. I processed these feelings by daily journaling and looking back at the entries, I tracked how far I had come in clearing the blocks that were holding me back.

My aim was to move forward and finally be visible to assist other people in breaking negative thought patterns that caused cycles of stress and anxiety. I knew that unlocking this approach would be the key to releasing the energy blocks that kept people stuck and repeating behaviours that hindered their healing. Recognising the deep emotional pain many were experiencing, I created a safe and supportive online coaching space specifically designed for those grappling with loss and loneliness.

This space became a refuge, helping people find their way out of the emotional chaos and overwhelming triggers that led to uncertainty and despair. Through compassionate guidance, they began to rebuild their sense of hope, discover new paths forward, and finally break free from the patterns that no longer served them.

Growing in confidence presenting online courses, challenging myself to stand up and be visible, and totally out of my comfort zone, I started to meet and take part in new business arenas, reaching bigger audiences than ever before.

I attracted clients who shared the same challenges I had once faced and overcome. Because I had already worked through these issues, I could recognise their struggles and help them heal.

When I committed to my passion, unexpected opportunities manifested, bringing into my life new situations and clients in the most unexpected environments.

Like one client I met quite unexpectedly when we came face to face in our masks, a chance meeting at the local supermarket during lockdown restrictions. It was a normal Saturday morning food shop. I had always been an early riser and continued to do my weekly shopping at 6.30 a.m. to avoid large groups of people queuing for food. I was standing outside the supermarket in the queue waiting for the store to open when the chance meeting took place. I was chatting to a lady in the queue called Lisa, we shared our stories about experiencing working from home, being in lockdown, wearing face masks and the progression of the virus that remained the topic of everyday news and conversation.

As we continued talking, I couldn't help but share my passion for helping others transform their lives. I spoke with enthusiasm about how I guide people to manifest their ideal life, find what's been missing, and experience lasting happiness. It turned out we had a lot in common, especially when it came to spiritual beliefs and our faith in the power of universal energy. We both believed that the energy we put out attracts the right people and experiences into our lives, serendipity in action.

Lisa, originally from the USA, had moved into our local neighbourhood in an apartment nearby to the town shops just before lockdown. We chatted until the store opened and Lisa asked if I would coach her; she wanted to lose some weight and wanted some motivation and coaching.

I gave Lisa my contact details and the following week we started working together. After our first session, I realised this was my aligned path

– it had ignited the familiar energy boost within me, confirming I was on purpose. My passion to work with and empower women, assisting them to break old patterns and create new realities, had now started materialising in front of my very eyes.

During the sessions that followed, Lisa revealed that she was struggling with financial debt. She realised her thoughts about money were unhealthy. No matter how much she earned each month, it never felt like enough. She kept spending more, sinking further into debt, and feeling increasingly lonely and empty inside.

As we delved deeper, it became clear that her emptiness and her relationship with food were connected. Lisa would turn to comfort food to feel better, trying to fill the emotional gap created by her financial struggles and guilt. Food and money gave her temporary pleasure, but this quick fix only masked the deeper feelings she was avoiding.

Despite these coping mechanisms, the underlying problems remained. Lisa's debt continued to grow, and her comfort eating left her feeling heavier in body, mind, and energy. Her self-esteem took a serious hit.

Once Lisa became aware of her emotions, habits, and behaviours, we worked together to challenge her thought patterns. By uncovering the limiting beliefs buried in her subconscious mind, she was able to unpack, start to heal and let go of past experiences. The outdated programs she held around food and money surfaced. As her mindset shifted, so did her energy.

Lisa began managing her diet and taking back control of her finances more effectively, setting herself goals and daily routines, focusing on her wellbeing and creating the right energy to manifest change.

Within just three months, new job opportunities appeared and increased financial flow came into her life.

Lisa's money worries began to fade, and with them, a new sense of lightness and control took over. She felt happier, more confident, and started planning for financial growth with clarity and purpose.

Instead of relying on unnecessary purchases to feel secure or happy, she embraced balanced, fulfilling daily routines that supported her wellbeing. With each step, she created a healthier lifestyle, built on intention rather than impulse. Empowered by the knowledge that true security comes from within, not from what we own.

Lisa's life blossomed as she let go of using food for comfort and refocused on reclaiming her sense of self. She began taking bold action, planning for the future, and writing a new chapter of her life.

With her mind reset and filled with fresh enthusiasm, she radiated an energy that attracted exciting new opportunities. One of those opportunities was the loving partner she had always dreamed of. Without effort, he stepped into her life, as if drawn by her new-found confidence and clarity.

At the end of our coaching sessions, I asked Lisa what her greatest manifestation had been. Without hesitation, she smiled and said, "It's the love of my life – my perfect partner."

She had the perfect soulmate by her side, a loving relationship where she felt valued, comfortable, and accepted in her own skin.

When we start to get to know our unique blueprint in the mind and soul, we create a relationship with ourselves and new possibilities open, it all starts with learning who you really are. The power lies within you.

Takeaway Lesson

If there's one thing I want you to take away from this story it's this: There is always a better way to live your life, just waiting, and it's never too late to change and create the life you want. I know because I've done it and continue to expand and grow.

I use my gifts to support thousands of clients I work with, honoured to be witnessing their transformation as they develop the confidence and belief to follow their true path and purpose in life.

My aim writing this book is to show you how you can do it too by finding the real power, the inner YOU, LOVE.

Chapter Eighteen
The Gift

Our most precious gifts – time, health, and wellbeing – are often overlooked because we assume they will always be there. But life can change in an instant, and what we have today might not be guaranteed tomorrow.

Practising gratitude means appreciating these gifts every day, being fully aware of the present moment, and recognising the value in what we often take for granted. By cultivating gratitude daily, we not only enhance our sense of fulfilment but also build resilience for when life's unexpected changes come.

I've witnessed the impact in my life many times with sudden changes in jobs and relationships, like losing my best friends, my dad dying, and changes in my husband's health and wellbeing.

Let me tell you more about Tony's background. He'd been born with only one functioning kidney and, in his early teens, the good functioning kidney started to fail, meaning he would require a kidney transplant. Luckily a living donor – Tony's dad – was a match and gave him one of his kidneys. Tony went back to living a normal life. However, after five years this donor kidney started to reject, and Tony once more had to go back on dialysis whilst he waited for a second kidney donor to match. A further six years passed. Dialysis was a main part of his daily life whilst waiting on the transplant list. Then the call came: a kidney donor matched and Tony could once more start to live life again, without the restrictions of the dialysis machine.

I first met Tony back in 2008. He had already had his second transplant which had been functioning well for over fifteen years. His condition never impacted or restricted our lifestyle or relationship in any way other than the numerous amounts of medication he had to take daily to keep everything balanced and to stop the kidney rejecting.

After being together for ten years, in May 2018, Tony and I married and had a wonderful small family wedding in Wales, Anglesey, one of our favourite places to go.

It was the perfect day in every way with our children to witness our happy day. Not long after our wedding, Tony started to get very tired and irritable, wanting to avoid thinking about the changes he knew were coming, and slowly, over the following months, he went into kidney failure. It was time, the decision was made for him, he could no longer continue to function normally and was strongly advised to start dialysis, or he would die. I then got to be a part of this experience and understand the impact and restrictions that kidney illness has on everyone who is involved and the changes required in lifestyles.

Three times a week, Tony had to be connected to a machine that filtered and cleaned his blood, doing the job his kidneys no longer could.

Each session lasted six hours, plus the travelling to and from the unit away from home. Valuable time away from family, friends, and each other became part of the weekly routine, along with fluid restrictions and diet changes essential to keep the body in balance.

Tony continued working part-time, and on his days off, he spent hours in the dialysis unit. He also went for dialysis on Saturday mornings at the hospital's day unit. For him, Christmas and bank holidays became just like any other day.

I am so proud to call this man my husband and he's my hero. He has such love for life and resilience, remaining positive throughout these major adjustments. Even through the tough times in lockdown and COVID restrictions, he continued to be fearless and carried on.

In May 2021, out of the blue, my biggest gift for him arrived. The Universe stepped up, granting joy and celebration, confirming the power of focusing and visualising with the power of the mind. I had been visualising and wanting this day to happen for so long and suddenly, my picture – seeing Tony back to full wellbeing – had manifested into our outward reality: The Gift.

In the early hours of the morning on the 16th of May 2021, a life-changing call came from the transplant clinic. Tony had been gifted a new kidney, the perfect match, and this would preserve his life, health, and our time together. There will never be any words to express how we both felt that morning.

I remember it vividly, a warm spring morning, still dark outside although the birds had started to sing, feeling both excitement and fear. We had been waiting for this day, hurriedly getting out of bed and packing his bag, getting ready to make our way to the hospital, having only a two-hour window to get there for the medical checks to be made to see if he was suitable and fully fit before the operation.

A million thoughts raced through my mind; we both sat silently as I drove him to the hospital for the early morning admission. I kissed and hugged him tightly, not wanting to leave and say goodbye. Such a rare gift and this experience was about to change his life. Eventually, I was told by the staff I had to leave the hospital.

Travelling back home alone, feelings and emotions of immense gratitude suddenly took over as my attention went to the spiritual soul who must have tragically died to donate this amazing Gift – a kidney to be used for Tony meaning he could live a normal life once more. I am forever grateful to this donor. Thank you.

Back at home, I felt lost. The day passed slowly as I nervously sat waiting for a call from the hospital. Later that evening there was still no call, and I couldn't sleep. I watched the hours on the clock tick by. Time had stood still for me.

The call came. Tony was okay. The operation had taken eleven hours of trying to manoeuvre and fit a new, third, kidney into an adequate position for it to function. Very little space remained inside his body – it was an already overcrowded area, with the non-functioning kidneys remaining intact, sitting like ornaments. However, with the skill of the surgeons, the positioning of this new kidney was successfully achieved. He now had five kidneys in total, I just hoped he could still breathe!

Tony spent the following three weeks in critical care as doctors waited and watched as the newly transplanted kidney bedded in. It was a very intense recovery time. COVID restrictions remained in place, so I was unable to visit throughout his stay.

Feeling alone, my anxiety levels raised over time, even though I had support from family. I just wanted to see for myself he was okay. After a few weeks in hospital and several bumps in the road, he came home. Remaining very fragile and weak, I was shocked when I first saw him, he had lost two stones in weight, unable to eat due to constantly feeling sick.

I remember thinking I would need to be creative in meal planning to get him back to normal, although when he arrived home in the early days of recovery the only food he felt like eating was takeaway burger and chips. Every day for the following month, I drove miles to the nearest Burger King, which apparently, as he informed me, had the best chips. Even though I had to pass three McDonalds drive-throughs on my way there, I would have driven anywhere and done anything just to get him to eat and enjoy the meal.

Eventually, the burgers became less attractive, and more home-cooked meals took their place, small portions increased over time as he slowly started to get stronger, recovering more and more with each passing hour and day.

I started to relax. I could sleep better knowing he was getting stronger with each day that passed.

Takeaway Lesson

When something major happens to a loved one, it's easy to focus solely on them – just getting through the day and making sure they're okay.

In doing so, I put my own work and wellbeing on hold.

However, I came to realise that taking care of myself wasn't just something I *should* do – it was something I *had* to do. By giving myself space, committing to routines that nurtured my mind and body, and staying present in the moment, I started to feel more grounded and energised. The shift wasn't immediate, but with patience, I learned that by letting go of control and trusting my intuition, the path forward would naturally reveal itself.

The truth is, self-care isn't just a nice idea, it's essential. When we stop forcing outcomes and allow ourselves to be present, we create space for clarity and inspiration. Sometimes, the best thing we can do is prepare ourselves for the right moment and trust that, when it comes, we'll know exactly what to do.

It's in those moments of stillness and self-compassion that we find our true direction.

Chapter Nineteen
Message Received

The Sign first arrived in September 2021, and it arrived during an early morning meditation. The Universe sent a sudden nudge, a thought and impulse flashed into my mind with the sudden urge to act. Write a book? What kind of book? I asked myself, as I felt goosebumps cover the whole of my body.

I'd always enjoyed writing in journals throughout and alongside my nursing journey and over the years it had been a good creative outlet for my inner mindset energy. So, I asked myself, should I use the saved material, years, and years of writing that had been stored in journals? All the random thoughts/feelings and intuitive messages that had come to me and I had downloaded into pages, but then I dismissed the idea from my mind.

The following weeks, each morning in meditation and carrying on throughout my day, I had the same strong thought and impulse to write a book. An extra nudge, feelings that almost felt like energy vibrating in every cell. The best way of explaining it to you is feeling like a sound, a subtle drum noise in my head, building louder and louder until a strong inspiration came over me to sit down and write ideas for a book.

This feeling was so strong it couldn't be ignored any longer. I followed my intuition with the feelings that seemed so intense and alive, I had to take this inspired action even though I had no idea what the book would be about or even how or if I could write a book!

I started with jotting down ideas on paper about my own life's journey. The more I wrote the more my energy flowed. My thoughts and ideas manifested into words and sentences to create pages, my story. The unfolding story of my soul's journey. I started to get the familiar goosebumps once more, an indication I was on the right path.

I noticed that throughout writing this book I had experienced and revisited my life's lessons that had been shown to me, unwrapping the feelings and past pain to receive the healing gifts buried inside.

Building resilience along my path expanded my awareness allowing me freedom to become visible.

I stopped running from my true self and embraced the reality I was meant to create, guided by a clear sense of purpose.

I'm here to serve and inspire others to do the same – to believe in themselves, to step into the light, and to unlock the gifts within them.

This silent partner within all of us, I had always felt my intuition, my inner being who came close and whispered to me in times of need. By starting to write, this energy poured out using pen and paper. I connected with this inner guidance, and I suddenly realised it had always been there, trying to connect all along my path. Always using the outlet of writing to express itself and communicate through me and to me by journaling.

Like the artist who expresses how they feel with the energy they use to draw, sketch, dance, or sing. It is the expression of the deep knowing from within creating the magic onto the big screen we all call our life's personal reality, this provided me with the deep sense of happiness that's been created from within.

By trusting my inner guide, I was able to create this book, finding healing and happiness along the way – my missing piece. Now, it's here in your hands, meant to inspire you and spark your own creativity.

Is it your time to connect with your soul's purpose and discover lasting change?

My mission is to guide you in discovering your path, finding your missing piece, and connecting to inner peace, all while embracing your own UNIQUENESS.

Our unique realities are shaped from the very beginning – through early childhood experiences, shaped by parents, caregivers, teachers, culture, and media. As we grow, we hold onto certain beliefs, choices, and rules, forming our personal reality based on the blueprint stored in our subconscious mind. This blueprint is like a photo album, filled with snapshots of emotions, thoughts, and beliefs – both good and bad – that shape how we see the world from the moment we are born.

All decisions are based on our unique programmes making everything we do and say fit a pattern consistent with our set of beliefs and our master subconscious programmes. The good news is we can change the pictures and programmes and delete old, outdated software.

Default programmes we can recalibrate and update. I went through my early life experiences without ever knowing there was a different way. I relied on the same thinking using recycled patterns from the subconscious programmes. I tried to make my external reality, including people in my life, work out or change so I could feel happy and safe, fit in. Eventually, I realised that I had a choice, and I could change my thoughts and create new feelings and manifest different outcomes. I then needed to work out the strategies and set goals to change my internal beliefs and external results.

Takeaway Lesson

Real change always starts from within. The outside world reflects what's happening inside of you, and only you have the power to make that shift.

So, when will it be your time to take control and create the change you desire? The first step is simple but powerful: take a moment today, close your eyes, and connect with that deep inner voice that's always been there in the stillness. Trust what comes up and take one small step forward.

The more you practise this, the stronger that inner connection becomes.

It's in these moments of stillness that your true path reveals itself.

Start now because the life you want begins the moment you decide to listen to yourself and take action.

Chapter Twenty
The Key Ingredients
to Make Lasting Change

Change isn't something that just happens, it's something we must *create* with focused energy and intention. Our body and mind are always sending out signals, like a beacon calling out into the world. In return, we get back experiences and information. But here's the key: it's not the events themselves that shape our lives, it's how we *choose* to interpret them. Our thoughts, beliefs, and emotions are the filters through which we make sense of the world, and they hold the power to transform our reality if we decide to use them wisely.

Every thought we have ripples through our entire being. One small thought can ignite a powerful emotion, which then shapes how we feel. Those feelings fuel more similar thoughts, and soon, our brain starts releasing chemicals that affect both our body and mind. This can become a vicious cycle if we're not careful with our thoughts. The incredible thing is, we have the ability to control this process. By focusing our energy on positive, growth-oriented thinking, we can shift the entire course of our lives. *It starts with a single thought.*

But what happens when stress takes over? When life feels overwhelming, our body kicks into survival mode by releasing cortisol, the stress hormone. Suddenly, everything feels urgent and chaotic. Our emotions are heightened, and fear or anxiety clouds our judgement. The longer we stay in this state, the more damage it does. Prolonged stress can trap us in patterns like obsessive behaviours or addictions, as we grasp for anything that gives us a sense of control or relief. But the more we lean into these coping mechanisms, the more we harm ourselves, physically, mentally, and emotionally. *This is where we need to take action before it's too late.*

Here's the truth: the energy we send out into the world doesn't just impact us, it attracts the very things we encounter. If we're constantly radiating stress, negativity, or self-doubt, that's exactly what the Universe will send back to us. Think of it like tuning into a radio station. If we're stuck on a low-frequency channel of negativity, we keep hearing the same sad song, day in and day out. The good news? We can change the station. *We just need to choose to tune into a higher frequency, one of positivity, possibility, and growth.*

This is the **Law of Vibration** in action. Everything in the Universe, including our thoughts, operates at different frequencies/vibration. And according to the **Law of Attraction**, like attracts like. Even though we can't physically see these vibrations, we feel them all the time. Ever walk into a room and instantly feel a "bad vibe" from someone, or catch someone's energy and feel instantly uplifted? That's the law of vibration at play. The question is: *what kind of energy are you putting out?*

So, take a moment to reflect: Are you attracting chaos and negativity into your life? Are you repeating the same patterns because your thoughts and emotions are stuck in a loop? Or are you consciously shifting your energy toward what you truly want? The choice is always yours but only if you take control of your inner world.

Here's the empowering part: **you are the creator of your reality.** The Universe responds to your energy, sending you the materials to either build your dreams or tear them down. But you have the power to change the blueprint at any time.

Throughout my own journey, I experienced the impact of this invisible energy. For years, as I've said previously, I was stuck in a pattern of low vibration, constantly fearing rejection and failure. My thoughts were rooted in self-doubt, and every relationship I entered seemed to confirm my worst fears. I was unknowingly attracted to the very experiences that held me back and kept me in my internal prison because, deep down, I believed I wasn't good enough.

It wasn't until I changed my internal narrative that my life began to shift. I realised that my self-worth didn't depend on climbing a never-ending career ladder or proving myself to anyone. Once I aligned my energy with my true desires, the Universe responded by opening doors I hadn't even imagined. *The change was real, and it was powerful,* but it all began with me making a conscious decision to tune into a higher frequency and align my energy.

Sometimes it takes a major life event to shake us awake, a breakup, the death of a loved one, or the loss of something we thought we needed. But here's the thing: you don't have to wait for life to force you into change. **You have the power to choose and change right now.**

The tools are in your hands. You can rewrite the story, shift your energy, and create a life that reflects your deepest desires. Don't wait for something to happen *to* you. Take charge of your energy and watch how the Universe responds.

As I look back on my own journey that has unfolded in these pages, I realise that every step, every misstep, and every relationship that felt like a detour was actually a lesson, a guidepost pointing me back to myself. For so long, I sought happiness by pouring myself into others, believing that by healing them, I would find the healing I so desperately needed. But the truth is, we cannot give what we do not have. Trying to fix others while neglecting my own wounds only led to deeper chaos within.

The relationships I chose, the ones I thought would bring me happiness, often mirrored the internal struggle I refused to face. I sought validation, love, and peace in people who were just as lost as I was. Instead of finding joy, I found myself trapped in cycles of pain, repeating the same patterns because I hadn't yet learned how to break free.

It wasn't until I turned inward, until I truly began to heal myself, that I understood what it meant to feel calm amidst the chaos. The peace I had been searching for wasn't in another person, it was within me all along. I had to stop looking outward for answers and start trusting that I was so capable of creating my own happiness, of being whole on my own.

Now, as I stand in the calm after the storm, I know that my journey is far from over. Healing is not a destination but a continuous process of growth, learning, and self-love. I've learned to embrace my own imperfections, to see the beauty in the scars I've accumulated along the way. And most importantly, I've learned that the greatest gift I can give to others is to show up fully as myself, healed, whole, and no longer seeking validation from anyone but myself.

So, as I close this chapter, I walk forward with a heart that is no longer burdened by the need to fix others or find happiness in external things. Instead, I carry with me the lessons of chaos, the beauty of calm, and the unwavering belief that my journey, no matter how winding, has led me exactly where I am meant to be. Right here.

In embracing my unique path, I also discovered my purpose: to help other women break free from the chains of invisibility and step into their power. My journey of self-empowerment led me to create a business dedicated to guiding women towards their true soul path, offering them the tools and support to find their own happiness and freedom. I've come to understand that the challenges I faced were not just obstacles, they were stepping stones that led me to this mission, where I can empower others to reclaim their lives.

Takeaway Lesson

We often fall into patterns without even realising it, and these habits can drown out our inner voice. When we stop listening to ourselves, we may start seeking approval from others or just try to fit in.

But I invite you to pause and ask yourself: where in your life are you simply trying to fit in?

You have the power to change, just like I did. It's simpler than you think, though it does take time, practice, and commitment. Change isn't instant, it's a process, like building a muscle. Just as your body needs daily exercise to get stronger, so does your mind. Every day, you must put in the effort to shift your mindset and create new habits.

When you're truly ready for change, you'll find the time to commit. Think of it like starting a new job or relationship. This is the most important relationship you'll ever have, the one with yourself. Once you show your mind that you're serious about transforming, the resistance will begin to fade, and each day will get easier.

Remember, you are a transmitter. The energy you put out is what you'll receive in return. Tune into the right frequency and your actions and thoughts will create the outward changes you desire.

So, ask yourself: *What kind of life do you want to create?* The power to change everything lies within you. Now is the time to act.

In the **Toolbox** section that follows, you'll find practical exercises to help you on your journey.

Start by being the cause of your own transformation and watch as your life becomes the effect.

You can create the reality you want, you just need to take the first step, and remember that nothing changes until you take inspired action.

The Chaos to Calm Toolbox

```
Mindset Change
Reprogramming
Keys to Change
Why - When - Action
```

⬇

Meditation instead of Medication

⬇

Ways To Begin to Focus The Mind

⬇

Box Breathing

⬇

Candle Gazing

⬇

Visualisation

⬇

Vision Board

⬇

Meditation & Visualisation

⬇

The Chaos to Calm Toolbox

| Positive Thinking |
| Affirmations |
| Self-Worth |
| Feng Shui |
| Journaling |
| The Chakras |
| Crystals |
| The Check List |

Chaos To Calm Toolbox

Mindset Reprogramming

Let's get started

Start to become consciously aware of what it is that doesn't *feel* right within you. Awareness is the first step to successfully changing that *feeling*.

Observe your daily routines and behaviours, noticing what the 'go to' rescue remedies are that you use in times of feeling anxiety and stress.

STOP and instead – Feel it to heal it. This can be challenging at first, but remember you are safe and in control always. You always have a choice.

Start by challenging those familiar feelings that arrive on repeat daily. Example: For me, I woke up daily with worry and anxiety, focusing on how to get through the day, without even tapping into feelings! I was detached from what was going on within me, I was living on the surface of life's events and chores.

Why do you feel that way – Look at the situations that arise in your daily life, what feelings are you avoiding and why?

Who or what saves you in these circumstances?

Me? I would react and escape reality with alcohol, smoking, or negative self-talk (complaining).

Revisit your day's events and journal or talk through with a trusted friend what you have noticed throughout this week.

What do you do?

By letting it flow into your conscious awareness, being present with the feeling, in the moment, you get to make space to let it flow, heal and release.

When I first consciously noticed my own toxic behaviour patterns, I was reluctant to change. I wanted to change yet remained fearful of the unknown, keeping my default patterns alive by telling myself stories like 'It's too hard' and 'I don't know how to do it'. Or 'I'm not good enough' or clever enough to make changes. Or 'I need someone to do it for me' – to take control and rescue me.

STOP – Catch yourself, when you very first wake up, challenge what you're thinking and how you're feeling. Replace unwanted negative thoughts as soon as they arrive. Let them go immediately. Replace negative with positive both in words and feelings and move your body!

Start each day affirming how you want to feel and believe you are the creator of your day. In the beginning, it feels very superficial and even impossible to believe that new affirming words will make any difference to your day.

That's because those old programmes are still very much in charge. Remember when you try anything out of your normal default patterns and comfort zone there will be resistance, like changing your diet and avoiding your favourite cake!

With focus and determination to have something new, you will change.

You can have anything, but you can't have everything; you can lose weight, but you can't have the cake every day as well!

You always have the choice of how you think and feel. Start by noticing your body language and the words you use to express yourself.

Words carry power out into your reality, they can create or destroy your day. Pay attention to people around you and how they talk about themselves.

Is it good and exciting or negative and biting?

Overcoming fear is a unique personal process.

Sharing my story with you or reading how other people changed their life, can motivate and inspire you to act for yourself. Or like me, and most people, you can wait until life becomes so painful that change **must** take place to survive. You always have a choice at any moment and can change your mind any time you decide.

Move from Fear to Love and see how you grow.

We are all living by our own rules and the beliefs we hold. Who programmed your life and why are you not living the life you desire?

The time is now for you to drop what is holding you back from finding your missing piece and your own unique path to happiness.

Let's look at How To with the Three Keys

Combining the conscious **Thinking** mind and subconscious **Action** mind to activate goals.

I've provided this grid to give you some guidance.

Sit quietly for **Ten Minutes** where you won't be disturbed. Take a pen and paper and choose one area of your life from this grid you would like to change.

Three Keys

Alone Time Self-Worth	Physical Wellbeing & Fitness	Financial Wellbeing
Family	PURPOSE True Self	Personal Growth & Development
Work Career	Relationships	Friend Time & Fun

Ask yourself the following three questions, consciously bringing into your awareness the questions and the changes you would like to see manifest.

The Three Questions
keys to open your awareness and change your mindset.

1) Why?

Dig deep and ask yourself: Why do you want to make changes in this area of your life, will it bring you more happiness, is it for you or someone else?

2) When?

Do you want to make this change? There is never a right time, there is only this moment, NOW, to start to create a different future and outcome.

Be flexible. What do you love to do? What are you good at?

Ask: What is stopping you, blocking your way?

Being indecisive is the seedling of Fear that causes doubt, turning it into more fearful thoughts and keeping you locked out of your power to create your desire.

Procrastination sets in and you stay the same, 'Safe'.

Are you pleasing other people instead of pleasing yourself?

What if you pleased yourself?

What if?

3) Action

Can taking an action step make your life easier? Ask: What am I **not** doing that would be easy to do?

Write down one small step you can take today.

Asking questions and becoming consciously aware, starts to challenge familiar comfort zones and safety behaviour. These have been on default programmes, and you have given the commands to the subconscious mind. At first, it will cause some resistance when you start. However, with time and practice, you can use small steps every day to build that intuitive guidance within.

Next, break it down into the following Steps:

Plan – Create – Prepare – Action

Plan: Visualising the picture in your mind of what you would like to see, and by using your favourite colours, it comes alive. Become aware of what you're thinking at that moment, how does it make you feel?

Create: Write it down or draw the picture to visually see it on paper, keep it where you can see it every day. Allow space every day to connect to your picture and the feelings of having it already in this moment.

STOP – Take a step back, observe, look at your daily routines and habits – are they working for you to create this new mind picture or do you need to change them? You need to make space for something new to come to you.

Prepare: To receive – have faith and believe it will arrive without any doubt.

Keep a positive attitude, reframing any negative thoughts or feelings that may arise; these are signs of old limiting patterns and beliefs that will be trying to resist change and stay alive.

Action: How will you take the next step and take action to move forward? It could be making that phone call, applying for that higher-paid position or starting a new business idea, or even moving out of that old relationship.

The following tools I've tested and anchored along my own journey.

See which fit for you in making the lasting change/s that you want to create.

Give them a go, let them assist you in becoming consciously aware and reset your thinking. Start building stable foundations to change, connecting to your inner soul's purpose and finding that essential missing piece that's been within you all along.

We are all different and learn from each other. Let me know how you experience these tools in unlocking your inner power and upgrading your mindset.

Repetition is the key to success. I recommend a disciplined daily morning and/or evening practice for commitment to change. Regular, daily practice will prepare your mind and train your focus.

Discipline is the key to success.

On first waking up or just before going to sleep are the two most fertile times to plant the seeds in your subconscious mind.

In the following exercises, you will be the attentive Gardener, fertilising the soil of the conscious mind and causing the flowers to appear over time – delivered by the subconscious mind.

Commit Time to create **Change – Consistency** is the key.

It's worth the investment of committing time to make the changes, or you can stay the same, remember you always have a choice!

Try each tool listed here for at least **30 days,** making it part of your daily routine.

The amount of time you spend on the chosen tool each day is up to you.

Daily routines become habitual over time and will rewire the subconscious mind with any good or bad daily practices.

Meditation instead of Medication

Power tool – If I could only offer one tool for you to try it would be meditation. It's FREE and you can do it anywhere, anytime, alone or in a group.

This powerful tool has been used for centuries by many cultures and in some religions in the form of prayer. It doesn't matter if you're religious or believe in spiritual, higher, universal energy. This is the universal magical energy and opens your conscious mind more and more to possibilities and expansion.

This practice changed my life, energy, wellbeing and awareness, from living my life in a state of anxiety, worry and stress, and having no direction or awareness of who I was, to finding my inner identity and gift, and who I really am. This one tool grounded me to connect to inner peace, happiness, wellbeing, and the abundance that now continuously flows in my life.

Simple to do, but so hard when you first begin to sit still and understand it's that powerful connection that runs deep within.

I first tried to meditate in my early 20s and with very little information available on 'how to', I gave up several times. My mind constantly wandered, and I told myself I couldn't focus, didn't have the time to waste! It was impossible for me – this was my story living on the outside of life in my own chaos and confusion.

Then the Universe sent me a new sign, I stumbled across an advert for a group mediation class, and this experience changed my life. Although it could have gone either way, I could have run away never to return. But I'm glad I stayed committed and I experienced the magic this positive energy flow gave me within my mind and body. My life would not be the same without it today. It's like reducing the pressure and plugging into the electricity of the infinite Universe charging portal. Charging up every cell in the body, every morning receiving the powerful charge, opening to feelings of happiness and calmness that is my inner guide aligning me in my life in the most positive way.

This probably sounds a bit woo woo and it did to me when I first tried it, waiting for that magic, but believe me when I tell you that the day will come when you do connect and drop into infinite fields of possibilities, and you will feel its true power. That's when you will understand your own inner power. And it's free for us all to connect to at any time, whenever you want to. Why not give it a try!

Remember, when you first start anything new it will feel uncomfortable and even frustrating. Like any new experience or habit, distractions from anywhere or everywhere will get the ego mind pulling you back into your comfort zone, moving you back into familiar, predictable, states of mind.

This is because the subconscious mind stores and retrieves data – like a computer, its job is to ensure you respond exactly the way you are programmed.

When you close your eyes to meditate and start to slow your breathing, you will start to get access to the subconscious mind, allowing your conscious mind to communicate with it in a relaxed and receptive mode. The attention and focus send a flow of energy, and then new information and ideas will filter through to the conscious mind.

This is the foundation.

Meditation will give you peace of mind each day and show you the way. Whatever you are focusing on and setting the intention to attract, open your heart with love and faith and your mind will start to communicate.

Meditation isn't only sitting still, crossed-legged, with your eyes closed!

There are many forms of meditation. Here's a list of examples: sitting in silence and watching a beautiful sunset; star gazing; dancing; listening to music; any creative project; martial arts; nature watching; gardening; and so much more. Anything that induces a 'flow state'. Relaxing your body and focusing your mind is meditative. Flow state is about being in the present moment. The power of NOW!

Mindfulness practice is 'flow state' – to notice without judgement.

If you are a beginner or new to meditation, I'd recommend you first try out the following tools.

These tools will get you ready, take you away from the chaos of the conscious mind, and will improve your focus and concentration, opening the mind to meditation and creation.

Box Breathing: First Aid for the Mind

Box Breathing can be used anytime and anywhere when dealing with stressful or challenging situations.

This tool can calm the body and the mind's reaction to a challenging situation and allow you the time to become grounded in the 'here and now moment', empowering you to respond in a more centred, controlled, and confident way.

There are many breathing techniques you can use and exploring different ones will help you decide which one best fits for you.

I'm providing just one popular and very simple breath exercise that you may wish to try out and see if it feels good to you.

Breath counting shows you that the mind and breath are interrelated and that one inevitably affects the other. You can use the breath to steady the mind. The mind can draw you along sometimes difficult pathways of the inner world. My experience of this was when I first started meditation in unfamiliar surroundings and experienced a panic attack. My mind was trying to keep me safe and telling me to run away, it was when I took a deep breath to prepare myself that I relaxed and centred my body and mind, and experienced the most amazing gift of peace and clarity.

The treasures are hidden deep within your mind. Over time, new thought patterns will create new ideas for life's problems, always giving you the right solutions.

Let's Begin

Seat yourself in a comfortable position that suits you and where you can remain undisturbed for 10 minutes. Turn off your phone and any other environmental distractions. Make sure you're sitting upright in a chair with your feet firmly on the ground and the temperature of the room is comfortable. Set an alarm for 10 minutes, a gentle-sounding alarm that will not startle you.

Now close your eyes and begin to feel the free flow of your breath. The breath should come in through your nostrils and back out through the nostrils. You will find that this method of breathing will be the most beneficial for inducing a relaxed body and mind to create a meditative state.

The Box Breathing technique is popular and easy to use.

The breath holds the mind in concentration and attention.

The goal is to keep the mind focused on counting.

> **STEP 1:** Take a deep breath in through your nose, counting slowly to four, and feeling the air entering your lungs.
>
> **STEP 2:** Hold your breath for 4 seconds and try to avoid inhaling or exhaling for those 4 seconds.
>
> **STEP 3:** Slowly exhale through your mouth for 4 seconds.
>
> **STEP 4:** Repeat steps 1 to 3 until you feel centred and completely relaxed.

At this stage, this practice is still concentration and not proper meditation. This is training the mind to concentrate on the breath rather than unwanted thoughts that may try to interrupt your practice.

Allow your breath to push the negative energy out of your body and mind. This is your first real test in concentration. By using your willpower, you can bring the mind back to the act of counting. That is all you need to do.

The first couple of times of doing this exercise it may feel forced and unnatural. Your mind will get upset because it's out of the normal routines and pre-programmes and that is normal but, like any new experience or exercise, continue to persevere and practice every day for 30 days.

I promise, after 30 days of practice, you will notice changes as you become more focused, calmer, and find it easier to concentrate. You will also feel more relaxed, less tense, and more peaceful as you go about your everyday life.

Candle Gazing

The human mind loves distractions. It loves to be busy, and it loves to feel important. It will often lead us down blind alleyways, try to keep us in the clouds, and play games that leave us lost, stuck and confused.

Candle gazing lights the way on the path, journeying into the subconscious mind. The candle gazing experience shows you the link between the mind and the breath; consciously controlling the breath can help you to concentrate upon just one object in this experience – the candle.

It is time to focus on the here and now.

Let's Begin

Candle gazing takes the practice of concentrating one step further. This time, choose a candle that you find pleasing and place it in a candle holder on a secure top, free of clutter, where it won't fall. Place it so it's directly in front of you where you are sitting in a comfortable chair.

Next, set your soft tone alarm clock for 5 minutes.

Light the candle and position it so the flame is as close to your eye level as possible. Darken the room by turning off any lights and closing the curtains.

The distance between you and the candle should be no more than two feet and no closer than one foot. Now, to begin...

Use the breathing technique you used for breath counting, only this time do not count the breaths.

Just allow the in-breath and out-breath to flow in a steady, slow, deep, and relaxed manner until you feel calm and relaxed.

In this exercise, all you are doing is observing the play of the candle flame as it burns on the wick. Gaze softly at the candle flame, allowing the eyes to feel soft, not hard or staring.

Begin to feel that, as you breathe, you are being drawn into the flame mentally, that is, your eyes are becoming more gradually attentive to the flame.

Slowly, as you use the constant rhythmic breathing to keep the mind and eyes focused gently upon the flame, you will find yourself becoming fascinated by the flame in front of you as it moves in little flickers and dances on the wick.

Now focus on one point of the candle, the white tip, or the yellow flame, or where it burns at the wick itself. Here comes the testing part, you must not move your eyes, either left or right or up or down. You must not let them flick away from the focus and onto any other objects in the room or look behind the candle in the distance.

You must hold your attention on the flame – only the flame – not the body of the candle or candlestick.

Holding your gaze steady, with soft eyes and regular breathing.

Try not to blink. If you must, there should be long intervals between each blink. This is virtually impossible for many people, and everyone finds this part of the practice difficult at first. But with continual regular practice, even the need to blink will naturally subside as you are drawn deeper into the experience. The candle-gazing experience can be meditative, even though it is primarily a practice of concentration rather than actual meditation.

When the 5 minutes of candle gazing have passed, immediately after your alarm has informed you that the session is over, gently place the palms of your hands over closed eyes (taking care not to press the palms onto your eyeballs) and watch for the afterimage to appear in your mind's eye.

Assuming the room was dark enough in your practice of candle gazing, the afterimage of the candle will register on the retina at the back of the eyes. You will see an image of a bright yellow flame. Now watch what happens.

The afterimage will begin to glow in a wonderful kaleidoscope of beautiful and fascinating colours. Seeing colour brighter than ever before, enjoy the moment. Candle gazing will assist you in your visualisation practice whilst in a meditative state.

Both box breathing and candle gazing tools can be used as exercises to train the mind for meditation. Only discipline and a firm commitment to regular practice will ensure success. You will be glad you stuck to it.

Be patient – anything new requires practice and conscious effort, but with time, you'll see the results you desire. Persistence is key, and the rewards far outweigh the initial challenges of building discipline.

Both the box breathing and candle gazing tools have been recorded and are available free to download. You'll find a link to my website at the end of the book.

When you have mastered the foundation tools of breath and candle gazing, you may wish to move on to combining meditation with breath and visualisation – that will now be easier to do.

Visualisation

Everything is created in your mind first before it is seen in reality, and you have to believe it before you see it. This powerful tool is used by some of the world's most successful people. Creating new pathways and rewiring the brain to achieve the desired goal.

Visualisation can be used on its own or combined with meditation to really double the outcome. It is extremely simple, and everyone can do it.

Visualisation Practice Using Your Senses

Close your eyes for five minutes and picture your ideal life, as if you're already living it six months from now. Imagine yourself in better health, feeling confident, enjoying financial abundance, meeting a new partner, or thriving in a dream job. As you visualise, engage all your senses to make the experience vivid and real.

What do you see around you?

How does it feel to be in this moment?

What sounds fill the air (perhaps people's voices, music, or a favourite song)? Notice the scent, maybe the fragrance of your favourite perfume or a floral aroma.

Finally, focus on touch, what do your hands feel as they make contact with objects or textures around you?

Allow your senses to fully immerse you in this new reality and create your unique mental image as real as possible.

Visualise exactly what you want to see, intensifying the feeling that you feel in this moment, creating the picture vividly in your mind, making it BIG and bright, turning up the lights. Act as if it is already here in your life NOW.

Worry less about how it will come, just be in the **now** moment, being careful not to let any destructive thoughts creep in, keep it positive.

Just before you go to sleep every night allow space to visualise your picture. This is when the subconscious mind is most receptive and will go to work making the picture whilst you sleep, it's a very powerful tool to use.

Imagining something clearly can turn it into reality. Your conscious mind works like a camera, capturing the image of what you want, while your subconscious mind develops that image, making it real – just like focusing on a candle during a meditation exercise.

Understanding the Power of a Vision Board

Another useful way of reminding you to stay focused on your goal is to create a vision board.

A vision board is a powerful tool that combines imagery, words, and affirmations to help you manifest your goals and dreams. By visually representing your aspirations, a vision board serves as a daily reminder of what you want to achieve. It helps keep you focused.

How it Works:

- **Imagery:** Images are a direct way to connect with your emotions. By choosing pictures that represent your goals – whether it's a dream home, career, or personal growth – you create a clear mental picture of what success looks like for you.

- **Words & Affirmations:** Positive affirmations and empowering words reinforce your new belief in achieving those goals. Phrases like "I am confident" or "I attract abundance" create a mental environment of possibility and success.

- **Subconscious Influence:** Positioning your vision board in a place where you can see it often – especially before bed and upon waking – enhances its impact. When you see these images and words regularly, your conscious mind begins to communicate with your subconscious, which is more open to suggestion when you're in a relaxed state, such as before sleep or upon waking. This helps align your thoughts, emotions, and actions toward manifesting your dreams.

Why it's Effective:

- **Daily Reinforcement:** Seeing your vision board consistently helps build focus and motivation. Your mind starts working toward opportunities **and solutions to make your dreams a reality.**

- **Positive Visualisation:** As you look at your vision board, you engage in positive visualisation, where you imagine living your dream life. This has been shown to reduce stress, increase confidence, and improve the likelihood of success.

By integrating images, words, and affirmations, a vision board becomes a daily tool for focusing your energy and intention. The act of repeatedly seeing these elements, especially at key moments like before sleep and after waking, gently programs your subconscious to align with your goals, helping you manifest them more effectively.

Meditation with Visualisation

SCRIPT (The Visualisation is available as a recording. Please visit my website to download it for free – you'll find the website address at the end of this book.)

The physical body must first be relaxed before meditation and visualisation can take place. Make sure you find a nice comfortable place that you can use where you won't be disturbed. Aim to do this exercise at the same time every day for twenty minutes.

Consciously relax your body and close your eyes, closing off your senses, this stills the activity of the conscious mind and gives permission for it to relax.

Now take a long deep breath, slowly in and out, letting go, relaxing with each breath as you continue the breaths, in and out as you go deeper and deeper into a relaxed state.

Tell your body to relax, you are in charge, and it will obey.

Relax every muscle in your body from the top of your head to the tips of your toes.

Focus all your attention on your right foot and feel it relax.

Next, focus your attention on your left foot, and feel it relax.

Now continue with this focusing on each part and feel it relaxing as you move up through the body.

Moving up to your right leg, to the calf muscle, relaxing the muscle, focus on your left leg to the calf muscle, relaxing it.

Continue moving up the body to the right thigh muscle, left thigh muscle, continue relaxing deeper and deeper, moving through each part of the body, relaxing and letting go.

Calm and relaxed, going deeper and deeper into your inner world.

Focusing next on the shoulders, neck, eyes, forehead, and top of your head.

You are now completely relaxed, and you are free from any tension in any part of your body.

Now, just continue to relax, let go and begin to focus on how very comfortable your body is feeling, you can just relax and let go.

Notice any sounds around you as you continue to breathe and relax deeper with each breath. Letting these sounds just drift into the background as you continue to relax deeper and deeper.

Releasing any tension remaining in any part of your body and letting go, relaxing your body and mind in this moment. Letting you go deeper and deeper into a calmness and deep relaxation.

You are now feeling so calm and so relaxed. Allow your inner mind's chatter to let go, allow the thoughts to pass through your mind like clouds in the sky passing by, relax deeper and deeper letting go, letting go, letting go.

Allowing yourself to be 100% in this moment of nothingness and space.

Not needing to be anywhere or do anything other than just relaxing right here and now knowing you are safe to do so.

I now want you to imagine and see in your mind's eye, (just above the bridge of your nose) see yourself floating on a vast ocean, feeling free, float deeper and deeper into the depths of your mind, now all you can see is space all around you.

A new journey to make, a new path to create starting today. Visualise new patterns and pictures that are taking shape in your mind. Create pictures – you get to decide those pictures you desire to see.

You are the creator of your life; you can consciously decide, and the subconscious mind holds the creative ideas and pictures to access your individual request to manifest.

With inner guidance, you are calling in the connection of the universal minds, materials to connect, guide your inner soul magic, given through your inner mind.

Stay curious and relax any thoughts, feelings or doubts that may start to come up, just feel them and let them go. From this moment on you get to choose good feelings in your mind/body as you connect deeper and deeper into warmness, like a warm relaxing pool covering each part of your body, relaxing you deeper and deeper, feelings of calm washing over you.

Now I want you to feel this feeling you have created, feel it as a colour, maybe it's your favourite colour, intensify the colour, feel the energy and excitement connecting and running through every cell of your body.

This is your colour to create and manifest lasting change.

Now breathe and start to create more and more as you travel deeper and deeper into the inner patterns, with information being given to you from the subconscious creative mind. Whatever you request and visualise will be created…

STAY here for a while and be open to the infinite possibilities in space and time…

After thirty minutes is completed, start to come slowly back into the room, feeling your feet on the ground, wiggle your fingers and toes, take a deep breath, and open your eyes.

Have a glass of cold water to drink, stay for a few minutes allowing your inner thoughts to surface, be open and curious about the ideas or prompts that will come to you throughout your day. Write and keep a record, watching the magic of the Universe start to unfold into your outward reality, connecting and communicating with your inner thoughts after each daily visualisation and meditation.

When you do this routine daily for at least thirty days, you will continue without much effort. As you repeatedly do something, your subconscious mind records that action and continues to play it at the same time every day as specified. It becomes a normal, daily, habitual routine.

The Power of Positive Thinking

The thoughts we keep thinking become beliefs held in our subconscious mind.

Think about your beliefs: are they aligned with what you want in life?

Once you identify limiting beliefs you can start to change them.

Whatever you are thinking and believing, positive or negative, your mind will find external circumstances to confirm you are right!

Early on in my journey, I started to use positive thinking. Every time I felt triggered by someone, my family or friends causing a negative thought, I would quickly notice and reach for a more positive thought.

By continuously challenging my thinking and beliefs about the situation I was in, I started to try something new. Noticing how I spoke to myself and others around me, I started practising being positive and life started to get easier.

I believed and expected better for myself, and it was delivered.

Watch your words, they have power to build or destroy.

By believing and practising on a deeper level of positivity my fear lessened, and my confidence grew.

I started using powerful positive affirmations, repeating them like a prayer. Over time, my conscious mind began to listen and accept these new suggestions. This process helped reprogram my nervous system, activating new feelings and bringing higher energy back into my body. It had opened the gateway to my subconscious mind, which does not analyse information like the conscious mind does, instead, it accepts repeated thoughts as instructions for shaping reality and new thoughts, beliefs and feelings.

As a result, I started to feel lighter and happier in my life.

By continuously feeding positive affirmations to your conscious mind, those thoughts eventually 'trickle down' to the subconscious, which stores them as new beliefs. Since the subconscious controls much of our behaviour and emotional responses, these new beliefs begin to reshape how you feel and act.

Your word is your wand, build it with strength to protect you; patience, and faith are the keys to creating.

My challenge for you:

Throughout the day, slip in positive and success-oriented sound bite words. Write it, draw it, speak it, believe it, FEEL IT. Notice what supports your new beliefs and consciously tap into how you are feeling about it.

Write down all the reasons for wanting this new belief before ending the day. After the full week, revisit the evidence and see how you feel.

Share your new creative energy with like-minded people.

Affirmations make a HUGE difference

Affirmations are simply formed statements that help you focus on a higher truth, a clearer intention and a greater sense of wellbeing.

We all spend a great deal of time lost in our thoughts, and if we don't live consciously, many of those thoughts can be limiting and prevent a joyful and creative life. Happily, no matter how many past moments may have been difficult, the next moment is like a blank page on which can be written a new thought, a greater action and a better life.

So, choose an affirmation from one of the lists that follow or create one yourself.

Keep *affirming* your truth to live your truth!

Mind Body Connections

Affirmations also impact the body through the nervous system. When your subconscious adopts new beliefs (e.g. "I am calm and centred"), the brain signals the body to align with these beliefs. This can lead to physical changes, such as reduced stress and increased energy.

Over time, the affirmation "I am confident" reprograms your subconscious mind to automatically trigger confident behaviours and feelings in situations where you once felt insecure.

Before you begin, take a look at the steps to set up your powerful affirmations.

There are three steps to successful Affirmation Statements:

1. **They must be personal** – use the words 'I' and 'My' in each case. For example, a proper affirmation would be, "I am confident when speaking in front of a large audience" **NOT** "You are confident."

2. **They must be positive** – you would state your affirmation like this: "I eat healthy meals every day" **NOT** "I don't eat junk food."

3. **They must be in the present tense** – logically you would think to make your affirmation in the future tense as in: "I will be successful in my business." But that is not the case because when you put your statement out to the future that is where it will stay. The subconscious mind needs to have tension to go to work and create the change you want to see in your reality. So, this example would become: "I am successful in my business."

Walking and Affirmations

Kickstart your manifesting, shift your energy, and start your day in the right way. Start a new morning practice that will put you in the right mindset for the rest of the day.

I do my affirmations when out walking because my energy is moving, and my focus is sharp and concentrated on my emotions. Bonus: Walking whilst doing affirmations gets your physical body in shape!

Look after your physical wellbeing, remember your body is the vehicle that will get you from A to B in life to manifest your success. Look after it and it will look after you.

Moving physical energy, in whatever way you can move, will change emotional energy (Physiology changes Psychology.) You can do affirmations on the bus, or in the car, the list is endless, and you can be creative with them. Remember repetition is the key to changing anything in your life.

Top tip: Write out an affirmation in a statement that is personal to you and fits your language. Try to make it like a rhyme or song.

In time, the subconscious mind will make it the prime focus and goal in the mind.

Affirmations can be repeated throughout the day, in any normal daily routine, when in the car, walking the dog or taking the kids to school. Talk to yourself with these powerful statements whilst shopping and watch how your energy shifts.

As I mentioned earlier, the most optimal time to do affirmations is just before you go to sleep at night and when you first wake up in the morning.

Mixing affirmations with visualisation will tap into feelings, triggering powerful emotions and bringing the picture alive in your mind whilst you sleep.

Start today.

There is one important added ingredient: you MUST believe you will receive whatever you request, whether it is financial success, health, love or a new career.

Try out the following affirmations or make up your own that fit for you.

Here are a few examples:

Affirmations to Receive the Flow of Money

- "I am successfully creating wealth every day in every way."
- "I am open to receive the energy of money."
- "Money comes to me in expected and unexpected ways."
- "I move from poverty thinking to abundance thinking."
- "I am worthy of making more money and money wants to be with me."

Affirmations to Manifest Love

- "I am open and receptive to give and receive Love in my life."
- "I am attracting the right person to me."
- "I am releasing my fears and embracing my future."
- "I am confident and full of joy."
- Affirmations to Manifest Health and Well-being

- "My body is healthy and my mind is peaceful."
- "All the cells of my body work perfectly."
- "I love my body and my body loves me."
- "My body is perfect just as it is."

Self-worth:
The key to living and creating a new Blueprint.

Remember, we don't create or manifest what we want, we create or manifest what we believe and feel we can have. If you are struggling to have what you truly desire, there may be some doubt or fear about what you *believe* you can have that's blocking you!

Our past beliefs about ourselves are deeply ingrained and shape our self-image, how we view ourselves, and our sense of worth. These beliefs influence everything we think we can or cannot do. They act as boundaries we've set for ourselves, often rejecting anything outside of them because it feels uncomfortable. We do this to stay in our comfort zone, where we feel safe and secure.

Be honest with yourself, real self-esteem and confidence depend on how you see yourself and what you find acceptable. It's about you, are you a people pleaser, giving your time and energy outside yourself? Isn't it about time you started to know your true inner self and find your own path to happiness that only you can create and manifest?

This is about changing yourself.

Self-worth is your
Net worth = Connection

My own experience of this was being in a lack mindset and poverty-stricken. All I could see I had created and yet at the time I had no idea. Back then I was a one-parent family struggling to make enough money to live and there was never enough. I felt like life happened to me, not for me.

One day the challenge came when out of the blue I received a gift of £100 from a friend who told me to treat myself. This was one of the most challenging and uncomfortable experiences of my life at the time. There were so many other things I could use this money on and yet to 'treat myself' I had not ever considered. I had ignored myself and my needs for so long; it felt alien to even notice and acknowledge myself in the mirror!

That money stayed in my purse for weeks. I felt inner power knowing I had the money yet uncomfortable knowing I had to spend it on me! In the end, I gave in and spent it on myself by buying some expensive perfume. Every time I smelt that perfume it gave me a warm glow inside and relieved the guilt I felt.

The penny suddenly dropped; I still had the same amount of money in my life, but I knew I was worth more. It was then I started to feel more abundant and worthy in myself, noticing my feelings and needs, opening up more to receive money which flowed into my life, slowly at first, from surprising people and places, and I appreciated it. Enjoying the lightness and joy I felt, it continued arriving, and I continued enjoying opening up with gratitude as it arrived right on time to meet my needs.

If this sounds like something you do – spending time and money on everyone except yourself – then I challenge you to start investing in your mind, feeling more abundant and valuing yourself.

Go ask for that pay rise or charge more for your time. You are worth it!

What do you have to lose?

Believe it and achieve it!

Self-worth Repair – give yourself some space to do this exercise.

I first discovered this power tool many years ago from Louise Hay's book, *You Can Heal Your Life*.

At first, it felt stupid to me, until I focused and got serious about finding the real ME.

Mirror work
Are you your own self-critic or creator?

- When you look in the mirror what do you see?
- Do you like what you see?
- What are you thinking and feeling?
- What is your self-talk about?

Mirror work

How often do you avoid making eye contact with yourself in the mirror, or only notice your reflection to criticise your appearance? It's time to change that. Start by offering yourself love and validation just as you are, in this very moment.

Try this exercise:

1. Stand in front of a mirror and look deeply into your own eyes. Hold that gaze for two minutes, staying focused on yourself.

2. As you look into your eyes, say out loud, "I love you." Use your name: "I love you, [Your

Name], I really, really love you." Repeat this five times.

3. Pay attention to what emotions arise. It might feel uncomfortable or even silly at first but stay with it.

Notice how you feel afterwards. Do you feel cheesy, awkward, or resistant? That's okay. The first few times I did this, I felt fake, like I didn't mean it, and I got distracted by flaws in my skin. But each time I stayed with it, I connected more deeply to my true self. If emotions or even tears come up, allow them. You might need to repeat this exercise several times to work through powerful emotions and connect to your essence.

This is a powerful tool to connect to your inner soul and really take a look at yourself – maybe for the first time.

At first, it will be uncomfortable and very emotional to connect within and find yourself, however, it will open your power to truly love yourself and will be worth your time, I promise.

Feng Shui
Audit Your Life

Feng Shui is an ancient Chinese art of arranging buildings, objects, and spaces in your environment to achieve harmony and balance, creating the perfect foundation for manifesting your desires.

It's also about self-care – protecting the positive seeds in your mind from external influences that could disrupt or destroy the new growth you're nurturing.

Setting boundaries is essential to safeguard these seeds of change. While it can be challenging at first, the growth that follows is well worth the effort!

I'm sharing this with you because this is what I did to protect my own growth. Sometimes when you want to change, close friends can get confused and want to stop you from changing, maybe convincing you it's too hard or a stupid idea that won't work. For them, it's about keeping you safe or stopping you because, if you start to change, they have to change as well or change their attitude towards you.

You may end up changing so much you have nothing in common with them. Are you prepared to grow apart from these friendships or have family connections that may end or become distant? It's up to you.

This happened to me with some friends and family members who didn't want to be open to change or understand why I wanted to change.

Instead, they would criticise or laugh at what I was doing. Sometimes this resulted in me stopping the changes I wanted to make to fit back into the friendship or family group, pleasing them and keeping everyone happy except myself.

Until it became too painful not to change, because deep within I had tried too many times to break away and decided I would never give up. I wanted change.

It felt like I had been locked behind a prison door for far too long, allowing others to hold the key.

It was time to reclaim my power. It was time to be me.

Here's what I did – give it a try and see how you feel after just one month of Feng Shui in your life.

Do a Life Audit

Feng Shui by Decluttering inside and out using the 3 P's:

↓

1) People

2) Places

3) Possessions

You are going to ask yourself three questions. Start with 'People', and then do the same for 'Places' and 'Possessions'.

↓

Keep

Reduce

Let them go

Take a pen and paper, give yourself at least 10 minutes, and audit.

List all the people in your life.

Using three columns, decide what to do with each relationship.

Change or temporarily reduce the time you spend with people in your life who don't support your new reality.

Notice and cancel out all the words they normally speak to you which are negative, or you hear from them that don't affirm your new beliefs.

Observing others and watching their behaviour, decide to move away from negative self-talkers that are stuck in mindsets you don't want to listen to.

Similar to bad news channels on TV or sad songs on repeat, change the channels!

1) Look at the People in Your Life

Ask yourself the following questions, who amongst your friends or family:

1. Encourages you the most
2. Cautions you the most
3. Discourages you the most
4. Helps you the most in other ways

Next, ask yourself do you want to:

Keep them in your daily life – they have good energy and you feel happier around them.

Reduce the time you spend with them – they bring negative conversations and drain your energy.

Let them go – completely cut the emotional and physical ties with them and let them go with love.

Keep

Reduce

Let Them Go

2) Places you spend time in your life

Places we visit often hold onto energy and memories of past events.

- Where do you spend most of your time?
- Do you need to move or rearrange furniture?
- How are you feeling when you are in that place?

Be kind to yourself and take some time out alone in nature and reflect on these questions.

Let go of any past hurts this may stir up in you, coming back fully into the present moment to allow space and create something new.

Keep

Reduce

Let Them Go

3) Possessions in Your Life

Possessions are personal and hold emotional memories, it can be tricky to let them go but action causes a chain reaction for change.

Remember, any outside action will free up internal energy that may have been stuck around that possession and memory, tied together in your mind for many years.

Freeing you to see things and feel things differently, you always have a choice.

Take your time and remember this is a work in progress.

ACTION is the key to your success!

Keep

Reduce

Let Them Go

Journaling Your Way to Clarity

This is the key to opening your inner power.

When my own life started to change, I became aware I could open up and expand my awareness through writing it down.

Looking back at my old journal entries, I can see how writing helped me in processing the changes that were taking place along my life's path.

Try it for yourself, it works, it's like looking into your mind – only on paper. It shows you where you are opening up to see where you want to go.

Start by journaling about what's happening in your life in detail, talk about your relationships, work, home, family, health, finances – anything that affects you or is the worry in your mind.

Next, write down what needs to change and the steps you can take to get there.

This approach is like goal setting: it will push you to do what's required to transform yourself for the better. It also provides you with a realistic picture of where you are. In that way, you're given the opportunity to course-correct to meet your target.

Cultivate an attitude of gratitude and combine it with mindfulness.

Every time you journal, list all the things you're grateful for. Doing this at the beginning frames the way in which you approach your problems.

Focusing on what you have in your life takes the focus away from lack and negativity, assisting you to create more appreciation for when new opportunities will arrive.

Gratitude will shift your mindset and positivity will become the normal expectation.

You can start each statement with this sentence "I am so happy and grateful now that I have ...." Open your mind to gratitude.

Putting your appreciation on paper cultivates a healthy habit, encouraging you to see the lighter side of life.

Take a mindful moment and make happiness a habit with a journal.

Reflect on all your favourite things, smile more at strangers you meet and notice their reactions.

Tips for Getting Started with Journaling

Make some time

Write but don't plan to write every day, writing once or twice a week is enough to develop a journaling habit, and you'll likely benefit from a relaxed approach. Start small, giving yourself 5-10 minutes of quiet and uninterrupted time is sufficient.

Start with a sentence such as: "Today I want to ...." or "I'm thinking about ...."

If you perceive that you have nothing to write about, write that sentence down. After a few lines of struggling to get your ideas out, the reason why you don't want to write will soon reveal itself. It's likely that you're running away from something you don't want or aren't ready to face.

I used to write whilst travelling on the train to work instead of wasting my time on social media and following someone else's story and life. I just wrote about my day and how I truly felt.

Use a pen and paper

Start small.

Writing by hand gives you a break from the screen, allowing your mind to unplug, it also allows your creative energy to focus a different way. Your brain engages with your hand and flows the energy on the paper, and your senses are used in the experience differently. My clients often remark that answers bubble up and spill onto the paper when they write by hand.

Begin with the date

This allows you to note the space between journal entries and you can also notice patterns and trends in your writing. My own journal entries gave me a deeper understanding and connection with feelings, and I discovered limiting beliefs that kept me safe. Later entries over the coming year showed how I had grown, changed my words, and unravelled my confusion on paper (like working out crossword clues).

Self-journaling is not for everyone. You could also try drawing the pictures that you visualise and create what you want to see materialise in your life. There are many ways to express your inner soul's energy and manifest the goals you desire into reality.

The Chakras: Seven Energy Centres

What are Chakras?

Chakras are energy centres in the body that play a key role in your overall wellbeing. There are seven main chakras, each located at a different point along the spine, from the base of your back to the top of your head. Think of these chakras like spinning wheels that help keep the energy in your body balanced and flowing smoothly.

The Chakras

Crown Chakra

Third Eye Chakra

Throat Chakra

Heart Chakra

Solar Plexus Chakra

Sacral Chakra

Root Chakra

Each chakra is connected to different aspects of your physical, emotional, and spiritual health. For example, the heart chakra is related to love and compassion, while the throat chakra deals with communication.

When your chakras are open and balanced, you feel aligned, healthy, and at peace. However, when a chakra is blocked or out of balance, it can affect both your mental and physical state.

What Causes Energy Blocks?

Energy blocks happen when a chakra isn't functioning properly. This can be due to stress, negative thoughts, emotional trauma, or even physical illness. These blocks can create feelings of being stuck, anxious, or overwhelmed. For example, if your root chakra (located at the base of your spine) is blocked, you may feel insecure or ungrounded.

Hormones, Endocrine System, and the Seven Chakras

Balancing Your Body, Mind, and Spirit

Have you ever wondered how your body and mind stay balanced? A big part of this comes from how your hormones work together with the endocrine system. Hormones help your body function properly, but they also affect your energy centres, called chakras. These energy centres help keep your mind, body, and spirit in tune with each other.

Have a look at how it works:

The Root Chakra – Hormonal Balance

The root chakra, located at the base of the spine, is connected to the adrenal glands, which produce hormones such as cortisol and adrenaline. These hormones play a crucial part in stress. When the root chakra is balanced it supports the healthy functioning of the adrenal glands, ensuring optimal hormonal balance.

The Sacral Chakra and Reproductive Hormones

The sacral chakra, situated in the lower abdomen, is linked to our emotions, creativity and reproduction. Reproduction in women is the ovaries, and testes in the man. Hormones like oestrogen, progesterone and testosterone are responsible for regulating reproductive functions and sexual development. By harmonising the sacral chakra, we can support the healthy production and balance of these crucial reproductive hormones.

The Solar Plexus Chakra and Digestive Hormone

The solar plexus chakra, located in the upper abdomen, governs self-confidence, personal power, and digestion. It is associated with the pancreas, which produces insulin, a hormone which regulates blood sugar levels. Insulin plays a vital role in energy metabolism and maintaining stable blood glucose levels. When the solar plexus is balanced, it supports the proper functioning of the pancreas, ensuring the production and regulation of the digestive hormones.

The Heart Chakra and Compassion Hormone

The heart chakra, positioned in the centre of the chest, is associated with love, compassion, and emotional wellbeing. It is connected to the thymus gland, which produces a hormone called thymosin which plays a significant role in our immune cell development and function. These hormones along with oxytocin, known as the 'love hormone', contribute to our emotional and physical wellbeing. A balanced heart chakra supports the production of these love hormones and enhances our ability to give and receive love.

The Throat Chakra and Thyroid Hormones

The throat chakra, located at the base of the throat, governs communication, self-expression, and truth. It is closely linked to the thyroid gland, which produces hormones that regulate metabolism, growth and development. The thyroid hormones such as thyroxine and tri-iodothyronine, influence various bodily functions, including energy levels, body temperature, and weight. By keeping the throat chakra balanced, we support the optimal production and regulation of the thyroid hormones.

The Third Eye Chakra and Melatonin

The third eye chakra, situated between the eyebrows, is associated with intuition, insight and inner wisdom. It is connected to the pineal gland which produces the hormone melatonin. This plays a crucial role in regulating our sleep-wake cycle. It helps us maintain a regular sleep pattern and supports restful sleep. When the third eye chakra is balanced, it promotes the proper functioning of the pineal gland, ensuring the production and release of melatonin at the appropriate times.

The Crown Chakra and Hormonal Harmony

The crown chakra, located at the top of the head, represents our connection to higher consciousness, spirituality, and universal energy. While it is not associated with a specific gland, the crown chakra influences the overall balance and harmony of the endocrine system. When this energy centre is open, it supports the optimal functioning of all glands and hormones, promoting a state of hormonal harmony and wellbeing.

How to Remove Energy Blocks

Removing energy blocks starts with awareness and intention. Here are a few simple ways to help clear and balance your chakras:

1. **Meditation:** Focus on each chakra during meditation. Visualise a specific colour (each chakra has a colour associated with it) and

imagine the energy flowing smoothly through that point.

2. **Breathing Exercises:** Deep, mindful breathing can help release tension and promote energy flow throughout the body. Concentrate on your breath while visualising the energy moving through the blocked area.

3. **Affirmations:** Positive affirmations can help shift your mindset and unblock stuck energy. For example, saying "I am safe and secure" can help clear blockages in the root chakra.

4. **Physical Movement:** Yoga and gentle stretches that align with each chakra can also help release trapped energy. Even a simple walk in nature can restore balance to your body.

5. **Healthy Diet:** a balanced diet is essential for hormone regulation and chakra health. Eat plenty of fruit and vegetables, lean proteins, and healthy fats. Avoid processed foods and excessive sugar that disrupt hormone balance and energy flow.

6. **Quality Sleep:** prioritise quality sleep to support hormone regulations and overall wellbeing. Create a sleep routine: aim for 7-9 hours of sleep each night.

7. **Chakra Balancing:** to remove blockages and rebalance the body's energy centres.

By regularly practising these techniques, you can keep your chakras open, allowing energy to flow freely and helping you feel more connected, grounded, and in tune with yourself.

Chakra Wealth Affirmations

- Root – "I am wealth."
- Sacral – "I feel wealth and abundance."
- Solar Plexus – "I do not chase wealth."
- Heart – "I love wealth."
- Throat – "I speak wealth into existence."
- Third eye – "I see wealth all around me."
- Crown – "I understand wealth is easy to attract."

The Power of Crystals

Throughout my journey, I've always been drawn to the energy of crystals. They've been a constant source of support, especially during times of low energy or emotional depletion. I carry them with me, place them in areas where I work, and keep them in spaces where I meditate and sleep. Their energy is grounding and revitalising.

Crystals are powerful tools because they transmit energy and can help us attract the right frequencies into our lives. Each type of crystal has its own unique properties, and different crystals are associated with attracting different kinds of energy – whether it's love, clarity, abundance, or protection. When used intentionally, crystals can amplify your focus, balance your energy, and help manifest your goals into reality.

Here are seven of the best crystals I've personally used to manifest my dreams:

1. **Clear Quartz** – Known as the "master healer". This crystal amplifies energy and intention. It can be programmed to help manifest anything you desire, making it an

all-around essential tool for your manifestations.

2. **Amethyst** – A crystal of protection and spiritual growth. Amethyst helps with mental clarity, peace, and deepening your intuition. It can guide you toward wiser decisions, helping to align your goals with your highest good.

3. **Rose Quartz** – The stone of unconditional love. Rose Quartz is perfect for attracting love in all forms – whether romantic relationships or fostering deeper self-love. It opens your heart to give and receive love in abundance.

4. **Citrine** – Known as the "merchant's stone" or the "success stone". Citrine is linked to abundance, prosperity, and achieving financial goals. It brings optimism and helps attract wealth and success by boosting your confidence and motivating you to take action.

5. **Malachite** – Often called the "stone of transformation". Malachite is a powerful crystal for deep emotional healing and breaking through barriers that hold you

back. It encourages growth and personal evolution, making it perfect for manifesting major life changes, such as new career opportunities or bold life decisions.

6. **Red Jasper** – A powerful grounding stone. Red Jasper absorbs and protects you from negative energies and strengthens your focus. This makes it easier to stay clear and steady as you work toward manifesting your dreams.

7. **Carnelian** – The stone of motivation and creativity. Carnelian boosts your confidence, courage, and energy levels. It's great for manifesting career goals or personal projects, fuelling your ambition and drive.

Bringing it All Together

When you feel it's time to take inspired action these tools will support you in manifesting your goal.

Try mixing and matching the tools that work for you and your lifestyle.

Make time, have space for self-care and meditate. Be in the 'here and now' space and time.

The answer you seek will arrive when your physical energy and resistance are lowered, and your mind is relaxed.

Opening higher frequencies for ideas to flow from within, just trust the process and let it begin, let go.

The world I see, I choose! Unravel the mind and you will find your true SELF.

Visualise – See

Ask – Listen

Feel – Create

Manifest Being Fabulous on Your Path (checklist)

Here are the checklists to keep you focused and on track, try the ones that fit into your lifestyle and feel intuitively right for you.

They are reminders about how to focus your time and mind to manifest your desires, finding your true path.

Fabulous unique humans, you are here to be, enjoy the journey and the path forward.

MANIFEST

M - **M**editation

A - **A**ffirmations

N - **N**ow in this moment

I - **I**nformation (internal/external)

F - **F**ollow inner guidance

E - **E**njoy feeling positive

S - **S**upport your self-care

T - **T**ime, free time – allow yourself time just for you, time every day to be with yourself.

FABULOUS You – Manifest through the senses the essence that creates your Uniqueness - YOU

F - **F**eel alive wearing colours that give you a lightness in energy and power.

A - **A**ffirmations that fit for you and your day.

B - Be conscious of what you think and speak, be kind to everyone, it will boomerang back your way.

U - Understanding unique inner patterns, what you tell yourself is true, failure or success it's up to you, be kind.

L - Listen to your body, use music to move your body and shift emotional negative energy daily.

O - Own the shadows and lessons you have experienced and survived.

U – Uniqueness, use smells that remind you of how to create your happiness and success.

S - See your creations on your vision board – create the pictures in your reality you want to see NOW.

The Law of Attraction through the above provides the materials to add, manifest and create when you start to take inspired action.

Let your new journey begin

My wish for you is to be happy and have your dream goals manifested into reality.

Let me know how you create your new unique reality.

How to Keep in Touch

Contact me if you would like to dive in deeper:

www.Soulpathfindercoach.co.uk

jackie@hello.soulpathfindercoach.co.uk

Follow me on social media:

linkedin.com/in/jackie-reeves-bbb93a20/

Facebook: @Jreeves8

Instagram: @soul_pathfinder_coach/

https://www.youtube.com/@jackiereeves334

TikTok: @jacjar8

About the Author:
A Journey of Healing and Discovery

I was that sensitive child – the one who could feel the world's pain, who instinctively knew how to soothe invisible wounds. My path took me on a winding journey of discovery, each career a stepping stone to my true purpose.

Nursing taught me compassion. Counselling revealed the intricate landscapes of human emotion. Hypnotherapy showed me the profound power of the subconscious mind. But it wasn't until I came home to myself – truly home – that I realised these weren't just careers. They were chapters in a larger story of healing.

I am an Energy Healer and Manifestation Coach, whose work isn't about teaching – it's about awakening. It's about helping you find that missing piece you've been searching for your entire life.

My mission is to help women like you peel away the layers of anxiety, societal expectations and self-doubt to reveal the brilliant, powerful woman waiting to emerge.

I'm not here to fix you. I'm here to remind you of the magic you've always contained.

Every woman has a story. This is where yours transforms.

www.ingramcontent.com/pod-product-compliance
Lightning Source LLC
Chambersburg PA
CBHW052012070526

44584CB00016B/1718